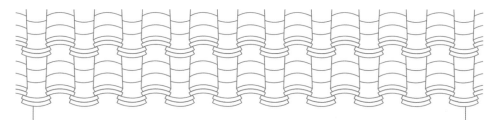

HISTORIC HOUSES IN FUJIAN

//////////////////////

• EARTHEN BUILDING

QU LIMING / HE BAOGUO

福建经典古民居

土楼

摄影 \ 曲利明

撰文 \ 何葆国

海峡出版发行集团

海峡书局

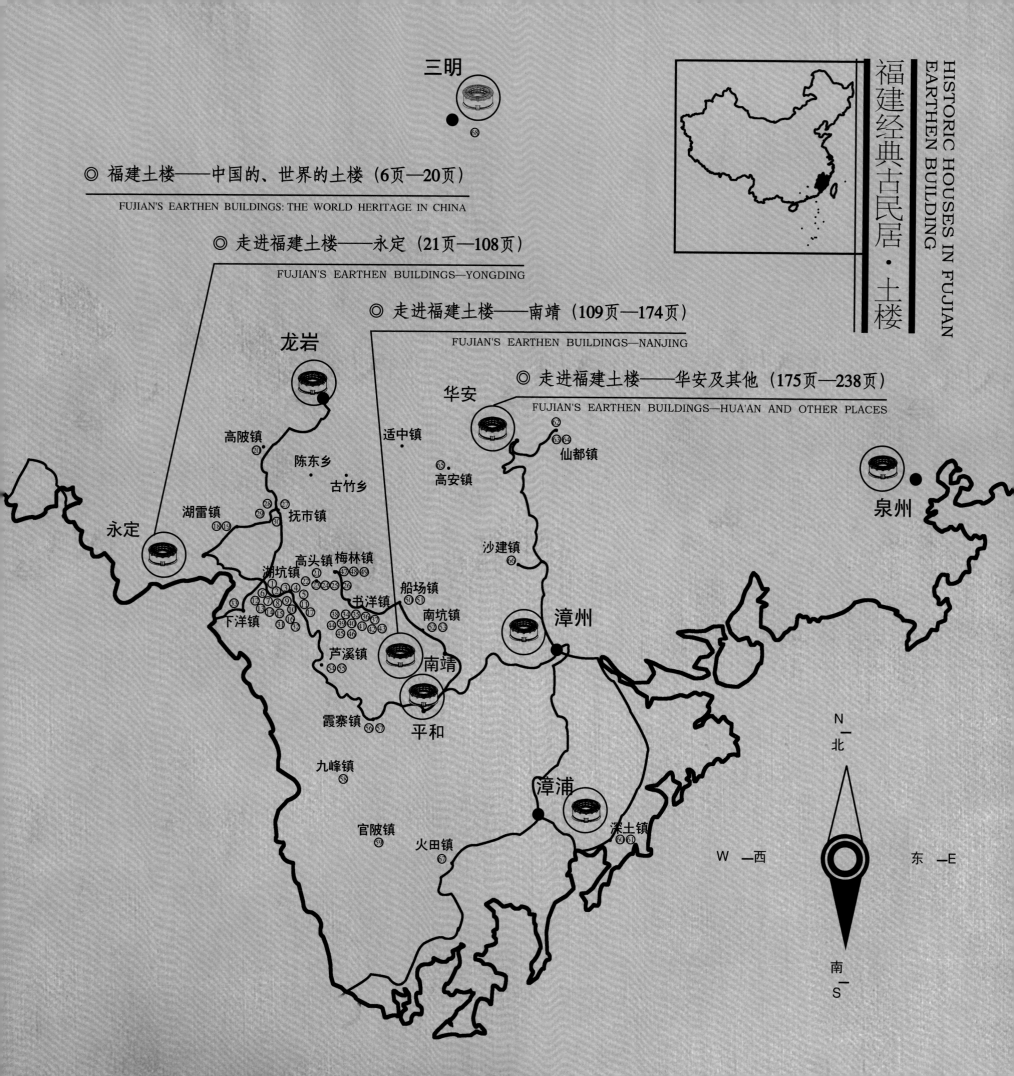

三明

福建经典古民居·土楼

HISTORIC HOUSES IN FUJIAN
EARTHEN BUILDING

龙岩

华安

适中镇

仙都镇

高陂镇

陈东乡

古竹乡

高安镇

湖雷镇

抚市镇

永定

沙建镇

泉州

高头镇 梅林镇

湖坑镇

船场镇

书洋镇

南坑镇

漳州

下洋镇

芦溪镇

南靖

霞寨镇

平和

九峰镇

漳浦

官陂镇

火田镇

深土镇

N
北

W —西

东 —E

南
S

田螺坑土楼群（南靖）| TIANLUOKENG'S EARTHEN BUILDINGS

初溪土楼群（永定）| CHUXI'S EARTHEN BUILDINGS

◎ 福建土楼——中国的、世界的土楼 ◎

● 何葆国 ●

2008年7月7日北京时间6点30分，在加拿大魁北克城召开的第32届世界遗产大会上，中国"福建土楼"被正式列入《世界遗产名录》。评委一致认为，"福建土楼"是东方血缘伦理关系和聚族而居传统文化的历史见证，体现了世界上独一无二的大型夯土建筑的最高艺术成就，具有"普遍而杰出的价值"。

数百年风雨沧桑，刹那间，以永定、南靖、华安三地土楼集结而成的"福建土楼"惊艳天下。

何谓"土楼"?特指分布在闽西南山区聚族而居，具有防卫功能，并且采用夯土墙和木梁柱共同承重的两层以上封闭式围合的多层大型居住建筑。闽西南土楼乡村处于福建、江西、广东三省交界地带，山势蜿蜒，峰峦叠嶂，土楼星罗棋布地坐落在山谷盆地之间。现存土楼最早的建于唐代（约公元769年），距今已经1200多年了，宋代、元代所建的土楼也有不少，明代的建筑则随处可见，最多的当属清代康熙年间至20世纪70年代所建。根据土楼的严格定义，目前有3000多座土楼被正式确认，列入《世界遗产名录》的"六群四楼"合计46座土楼，无疑是其中最杰出的代表。它们是：永定县的初溪土楼群（包括集庆楼、余庆楼、绳庆楼、华庆楼、庚庆楼、锡庆楼、福庆楼、共庆楼、藩庆楼、善庆楼10座土楼）、洪坑土楼群（包括光裕楼、福兴楼、奎聚楼、福裕楼、如升楼、振成楼、庆成楼7座土楼）、高北土楼群（包括承启楼、世泽楼、侨福楼、五云楼4座土楼）和衍香楼、振福楼，南靖县的田螺坑土楼群（包括步云楼、瑞云楼、和昌楼、振昌楼、文昌楼5座土楼）、河坑土楼群（包括朝水楼、阳照楼、永盛楼、绳庆楼、永荣楼、永贵楼、裕昌楼、春贵楼、东升楼、晓春楼、永庆楼、裕兴楼、南薰楼13座土楼）和怀远楼、和贵楼，华安县的大地土楼群（包括二宜楼、南阳楼、东阳楼3座土楼）。永定与南靖交界，南靖和华安接壤，这三个毗邻的县份，行政上隶属于龙岩市和漳州市，在文化上有差异，也有融合，呈现出丰富的文化多样性。

当你来到土楼乡村，只见大大小小或圆或方的土楼、蓝天白云、青山绿水、茂林修竹、飞鸟野花、层层梯田、阵阵林涛、潺潺小溪、缕缕炊烟，完美和谐地融为一体，充满着田园牧歌的诗情画意。

当你走进土楼，你首先感觉到这是一个巨大的家族之城，然后你才看到一个个单独的家。

每一座土楼都有一个名字，大都取自族谱里的祖训，或者用祖宗的名字命名，用以励志、纪念，同时表达一种吉祥如意的心愿。楼门两边是一对楹联，大

都是楼名的藏头联，寓意深远。

土楼的形状主要有圆形、方形、五凤形，另外还有椭圆形、八卦形、半月形、交椅形等等，同一种形状里又有着不同的变化，可谓千姿百态各具特色，但却又有着明显的共性。

在客家人的词汇里，圆形土楼叫做"圆寨"，一个"寨"字可以让人遐想无穷，村寨、山寨……总之是又庞大又险要。在各种形状的土楼里，圆楼无疑是最让人感到神秘与奇特的。几乎所有的圆土楼都只有一个大门，大门一关，里面自成一个世界，外面的一切便全被挡住了。两扇大门板又厚又高，通常还包着铁皮，像是两个身穿盔甲的守门武士，五六岁的孩子站在门边，常常使尽吃奶的力气也无法推动大门。如果你要问圆楼的墙有多厚，你只要想想墙上面可以摆放一张八仙桌就知道了。

走进大门，是圆楼的楼门厅，这里是全楼的出入通道和休闲场所，两边通常放着长长的木凳，人们闲暇之时可以坐在这里聊天。年深月久，这长长的木凳被屁股磨得光亮可鉴。不少楼门厅还放着米碓、谷砻、石磨和糍粑臼等等，于是便会有这样的景观：妇女在舂米或者磨面，发出一种富有韵律的声音，男人则在谈天说地指点江山。

走过楼门厅，两条廊道分向两边，像是两只长长的手臂，把所有的同样形状同样大小的房间搂成了一个圆圈。一楼是灶间，对外不开窗，对内则用木构直棂窗，一般开得很大，足够采光通风。窗下通常设置有木柜，里面养鸡养兔，上面坐人，一物

两用。二楼用来贮藏粮食和堆放农具，俗话叫"禾仓间"。三楼以上是卧室，也只有从三楼开始，对外才开了一扇长条形的小窗户。

圆楼的楼梯最少有两部，一般会有四部公用楼梯，布置在与门堂轴线垂直的横轴两端。平和、华安两地的许多圆楼虽然格局相似，但因楼上不设回廊相通，家家户户都有一部独立的楼梯。

楼里的天井至少有一口井，妇女们在井台四周一边洗菜洗衣，一边闲扯拉呱，这里是土楼里又一个人气旺盛的地方。

圆楼的一层，与大门相对的敞厅是祖堂，供奉着祖先牌位，是家族祭祖和议事的地方。在较大的圆楼，天井中心位置往往建造一座四方形的四架三间两堂式祠堂，既做家庙又做家族"议会"，也兼做学堂。如果是两环和两环以上的圆楼，那么楼内又是另一番景象了。多环式圆楼就是在圆心上大环套小环，环环相套，形成楼中楼的奇特情景。

有圆楼的村落，必定有方形土楼。客家人把方形土楼叫做"四角楼"，除了方与圆在外观上的截然不同，方楼的内部格局跟圆楼并没有太大的差别。

五凤楼，是土楼另一种常见的类型。它层层叠叠，高低错落，看起来犹如一片壮观的府第、宫殿，内部装饰颇为讲究，很多人第一次走进五凤楼，总掩饰不住一种惊讶：过去的山村乡民竟然也有这般豪华气派的住家？五凤楼的造型以三堂为中轴核心，左右有平衡对称的厢房，厢房的规模大小则视楼主的财力而定，有三堂二横式、三堂四横式、三堂六横式等

等。五凤楼的九脊顶坡度平缓柔和，风格朴实而气势非凡，呈现出汉代宫殿屋顶的显著特色。屋脊装饰更是考究而精致，两端翘成牛角或凤尾燕尾的形状，用生铁铸作两端脊尾的骨架，外以石灰泥成形。整条屋脊漆成彩色，绘制着孔雀、凤凰等瑞兽祥鸟和花草图案，和宫殿屋脊几乎没有两样。五凤楼大门前必定有一片宽阔的禾坪和一口半月形的水池，房子必定是前低后高、中间高两边低。也许这样说来有些抽象，如果你抬头看看五凤楼的屋脊，那飞檐往上高高翘起，不正像是展翅欲飞的凤凰吗？

为什么这块土地上会出现如此神奇雄伟的夯土建筑？为什么如此神奇雄伟的夯土建筑会出现在这块土地上？这实际上是同一个命题，我们不得不把目光投向历史的深处……

永嘉之乱、唐末兵燹、宋室倾覆，客家先民几度举族南迁，辗转吴楚，流徙皖赣。从动荡的中原几经流徙多方辗转，一支支客家人群先后来到了山高水长、偏安一隅的闽西南乡村。

一个敢于放逐自己的族群，一个敢于踏上茫然不测的逃生之路的族群，无疑是一个堂堂的族群。

在闽西南崇山峻岭之中，饱经沧桑的客家人找到了他们新的家，他们搭起了木棚房、茅草屋，终于可以歇下脚来缓一口气了。

就像一颗生命力顽强的松树种子，在哪里都可以发芽、生根、长成大树，客家人就是这样一颗种子，被命运的风吹落在异地的穷乡僻壤，没有怨言，只有感恩，它悄悄地从土地里钻出头来，在风雨雷电之中

苗壮成长，根系向四周伸展并深深地扎入大地。

安宁的环境，丰饶的土地，坚韧的意志，团结的精神，艰苦的劳作……客家人渐渐发展壮大。

人丁兴旺，自古是中国人对家族的祈愿。一支支客家人家族在人口猛长的势头面前，又出现了一个困扰的难题：居住。

安居乐业，这是最朴素也是最迫切的要求。

老人们难忘中原祖地那深宅大院，可是往事依稀，繁华不再，他们日思夜想的是，如何在这已经注定的地方安居乐业，不仅仅让整个家族有一个遮风避雨的结实户所，更让整个家族有一个凝聚人心振奋精神的灵魂家园。

现在谁也无从考证，第一个发明土楼的客家人是谁。实际上，土楼也不是具体哪个人发明的。土楼是客家人迷恋历史的情愫、超凡脱俗的天才想象和山村现实的物质条件相结合的产物。可以肯定，第一座土楼很粗陋，很不成熟，甚至有可能是很可笑的。然而在漫长的岁月里，客家人不断积累经验，不断努力创造，夯土技术越来越高超，审美境界越来越开阔，土楼也就造得越来越高、越来越大、越来越美——犹如一只丑小鸭，终于变成了天鹅。

客家人从远处走来，又不断地向远处走去。他们走在路上的身影正是中华民族几千年来奋斗不息的写照。随着客家许多家族的继续迁移，土楼也从闽西南传入了其他地区。

客家南迁史，实际上也是一部汉族南迁史。中原汉族南迁主要以家族血缘群体为单位，整个过程是持

续不断的，迁移地域渐次推移，客家文化正是在这迁移之中和定居之后，逐渐酝酿、形成和发展起来。

作为客家文化的结晶，土楼并非横空出世，它的出现首先必须具备几个条件：强大的家族凝聚力、相对安宁的生活环境、较为雄厚的物质基础。

从烽火连天的中原南迁定居之后，客家先民拥有了一片宁静的天空。经过几代人的繁衍和拓展，客家人口迅猛增长，也积累了不少财物。只有在这时候，他们才有可能考虑，如何以血缘聚居的模式建造一座巨宅？

客家来自中原。客家土楼的造型艺术和夯土技术，无疑也是来源于中原。在西安半坡村和临潼姜家寨等原始氏族社会的遗址上，可以发现土楼造型艺术的原始形式；在黄河中下游龙山文化父系氏族公社时期的遗址上，也有大量的圆形与方形的建筑。随着私有制的形成和家族的壮大，开始形成一种"制如明堂"的建筑。明堂是中国传统民居"四架三间"造型的源头，而五凤楼的基本构成，正是"四架三间"。夯土技术何时在中国出现，尚难定论，但是在距今五六千年的古文化遗址，已经可以看到夯土台实物。商朝的夯土技术相当发达，奴隶主的宫室、陵墓和城墙，台基都是夯土而成的。历代的筑城、筑堤坝和建房，都广泛使用夯土。到了北宋，夯土技术又有了进一步的提高，在当时最权威的建筑工程技术专著《营造法式》和《筑城法式》里，都对夯土技术做了记述。明朝以来，夯土而成的民居，在全国各地普遍出现，土楼只不过是其中把夯土技术推向登峰造极的一

种民居。

当然，土楼的造型艺术和夯土技术在传承的过程中，发生了变异，这也是每一种文化传播必然遇到的正常现象，人类学家认为，"文化的变异是一种适应性变化，并且是通过世袭遗传的基础进行的。"客家人在闽西南山区建造土楼，正是适应了当地的自然地理特点。

土楼墙厚楼高，十分坚固，具有良好的防卫功能，于是不少人便想当然地以为，建造土楼完全是为了防卫的需要。固然土楼有着较强的防御功能，但事实上，土楼最早在闽西南山区出现，不是因为此地盗匪横行，恰恰相反，和闽南沿海地区相比，闽西南山区的社会环境较为安宁，人们安居乐业，才能逐渐积累财富，用几年、十几年甚至几十年的时间，夯起耗资巨大的土楼。闽南沿海地区历史上一直是海盗重灾区，明末清初更是战争不断，郑成功在此和清军进行持久战，无数村庄毁于兵火，老百姓流离失所，大量迁往台湾和东南亚。从明永乐初年到清嘉庆年间，在这漫长的四百多年里，闽南沿海地区每三四年就出现一次普遍的自然灾害，不是水灾就是旱灾，导致百姓要么颗粒无收要么无法耕种。与之相比，闽西南山区的山高水长环境和山田农业模式，便显示出其极大的优越性。如果说到防御的需要，那么闽南沿海地区的百姓无疑最需要建造土楼来保护自己，但实际上，他们已无暇自保难于生存，如何能够建成巨大的土楼呢？这一地区的土楼大多是清康熙末年之后建造的，而且大多为

客家人或客家人后裔所建。

由于土楼客观上具有防卫功能，也许比较晚近的某些村落建造土楼，确是出于防卫的需要，有人以偏概全得出"建造土楼是防卫需要"的结论，其实是只见树木，不见森林。防卫是所有建筑固有的功能。如果盗匪横行，洗劫一个村落也就是一朝一夕的事情，而土楼是不可能在一夜之间建成的，它需要一个漫长的过程，财物早被抢光了，如何还能建得起庞大的楼宇？

土楼雄伟壮丽，其庞大的规模远远超出其他地区的普通民居。历代政权对住宅的楼层数、房间数、屋顶形式、雕饰等等都有具体的规定，根据社会政治地位划分成各种等级。为什么闽西南乡村会有这样明显越规出格的土楼？有人便说是永定有一余姓女子，被明朝皇帝选为娘娘，深受宠爱，特地赐准她的家乡百姓可以建造四到五层的府第式楼房。这全然是无稽之谈，各种志书上均无此记载，要是真有其事，当地志书是绝对不会放过的，而且土楼早在明朝之前就已出现。这个语焉不详的传闻透露出来的奴性意识，实际上抹杀了客家先民创建土楼的气魄与才能。闽西南乡村地处偏僻，所谓"山高皇帝远"，王法有所不及，官方的住宅等级制度难以得到落实。在元代和清代，非汉人执掌政权，或许一向以纯正汉人自居的客家人不愿臣服，敢于超越有关的规定。

土楼表现出来的向心性、匀称性和前低后高的特点，以及血缘性聚族而居的特征，正是儒家文化和道家文化的一个缩影。土楼有形的基础是石块，无形的基础就是千百年来植根于中华民族之中的儒、道传统思想观念，这坚实强大的基础擎起了世界上独一无二的奇观。

儒道追求天、地、人"三才"合一，这是中国传统文化最典型的特征，这种思维模式在土楼里表现得最为鲜明，最为强烈，这也正是土楼不可替代的独特价值。

圆楼的造型模式与天地人合一模式，是同圆心的重合。风水师称土楼的天井为内太极或天池，客家人也常常把天井叫做天池，这种看似集体无意识的称呼，实际上反映了土楼对太极阴阳思维模式的仿效。如果以八卦形式来设计圆楼的内部空间，其造型图式与天地人"三才"合一模式的重合更是天衣无缝。

方楼的内部空间实际上和圆楼一样，也是匀称划分的，与圆楼造型同出一源。五凤楼的情形就要复杂一些了，但是，它的完整造型也是圆形的。人们往往只看到有墙有屋顶的部分，而没有注意其前后不可缺少的池塘和"围龙"化胎（或屋后弧形伸手），一叶障目而未能发现它的整体造型。实际上，五凤楼的池塘和"围龙"或屋后伸手，是前后对应、阴阳配置的。它们使五凤楼的整体造型，构成一个完整的圆形，生动形象地表现出"三才"合一的思维模式。

日本教授茂木计一郎曾经提出，"圆形土楼是母性，很像吞容一切的子宫"。与圆楼相比，五凤

楼更像是一个孕育生命的子宫，它前面的半圆形池塘，象征太极阴阳化生图属阴的一仪，活像是充满羊水的子宫的一半；"围龙"或屋后伸手则象征着阳精生气。以三堂两横的标准五凤楼为例，后堂是胎头，中堂是心脏，下堂是命门，上、中、下三焦之气贯通无阻，两横为手脚肢节，这就像是充满生机活力的一个人。

天地人之中的人，正是在土楼里实现了和天地阴阳的沟通。"三才"合一，这也正是中国人所追求的最高的理想境界。土楼达到了这一境界。作为一种形式与思维、物质与精神的产物，它表现出中国传统文化博大精深的内涵，使其本身超越了住宅的局限性，从而成为文化的一部分。其实土楼就是一个生生不息的文化圈，如此浩博精妙，它已不仅仅是一种民居，和闽西南客家人、闽南人的生活息息相关，密不可分。在土楼里安居乐业的子民们，他们日常的生活里洋溢着丰富的人文气息，使坚硬的土墙也变得温情脉脉。对他们来说，土楼已不仅仅是一个遮风挡雨的场所，而是一片精神的家园、一个灵魂的象征和一种文化的代表。对所有游客来说，土楼则是一道生生不息的鲜活飞扬的人文风景。

土楼文化是民族的，因而也是世界的。在全球化的影响下，如何保护民族文化的独特性，坚守民族文化的完整性，这对土楼来说同样是具有挑战性的话题。越是民族的，越是世界的，土楼作为世界人民共享的文化遗产，它的价值将被越来越多的人所认识。在中国的闽西南山区，土楼已经屹立数百年了，我们希望它继续屹立在不尽的岁月里……

FUJIAN'S EARTHEN BUILDINGS: THE WORLD HERITAGE IN CHINA

• He Baoguo •

At the thirty-second World Heritage convention, held July 7, 2008, in Quebec, forty-seven entries from forty-one countries were considered for World Heritage status. Fujian's "earthen buildings" (Hakka houses) were among the twenty-seven that were ultimately selected. The judges were unanimous in saying that the "earthen buildings" bear witness to the history of Asian clan culture and uniquely embody the highest artistic skill in rammed-earth construction. They have "universal and unique value." Not a single vote was cast against granting them this honor.

After centuries of endurance, the Fujian "earthen buildings"—concentrated in Yongding, Nanjing, and Hua'an-astonished the world overnight with their beauty.

Let me begin by defining "earthen buildings." The term refers to those large farmhouses where an entire clan lives together—homes particularly noteworthy for their defense function. With their rammed-earth walls and wooden beams and posts, these large homes-each at least two stories high—closed out the surrounding area. The southwestern Fujian villages with earthen buildings are located in the region where Fujian, Jiangxi, and Guangdong meet. In the boundless mountain terrain, the earthen buildings are scattered like stars in the valleys. The earliest extant earthen building was constructed in 769 during the Tang dynasty; quite a few were also constructed during the Song and Yuan dynasties. Those built during the Ming dynasty can be seen everywhere. Most, however, date from the late 17th Century to the 1970s. Using the strict definition of earthen buildings, more than three thousand earthen buildings have been formally acknowledged. Among them, the "six complexes and four buildings" comprising forty-six earthen buildings chosen for World Cultural Heritage status are doubtless the best. They are: Yongding county's Chuxi complex (including the Jiqing, Yuqing, Shengqing, Huaqing, Gengqing, Xiqing, Fuqing, Gongqing, Fanqing, and Shanqing buildings); the Hongkeng complex (including the Guangyu, Fuxing, Kuiju, Fuyu, Rusheng, Zhencheng, and Qingcheng buildings); the Gaobei complex (comprising the Chengqi, Shize, Kuafu, and Wuyun buildings); and the Yanxiang and Zhenfu buildings; Nanjing county's Tianluokeng complex (including the Buyun, Ruiyun, Hechang, Zhenchang, and Wenchang buildings); the Hekeng complex, also in Nanjing county, comprising the Chaoshui, Yangzhao, Yongsheng, Shengqing, Yongrong, Yonggui, Yuchang, Chungui, Dongsheng, Xiaochun, Yongqing, Yuxing, and Nanxun buildings. Also in Nanjing county are the Huaiyuan and Hegui buildings. In Hua'an county is the Dadi complex (including the Eryi, Nanyang, and Dongyang buildings). Yongding and Nanjing share a boundary, as do Nanjing and Hua'an. These three counties, administered by Longyan and Zhangzhou municipalities, show rich cultural diversity.

When you arrive at a village of earthen buildings, you see many circular and square earthen buildings of various sizes, the blue sky and white clouds, mountains and water, trees and bamboo, birds and wildflowers, terraced fields, small creeks, and smoke from kitchen chimneys, all blended together in perfect harmony and filled with a sense of poetry and painting.

When you enter an earthen building, you sense first that this is a large clan city, and only later do you notice that it consists of many single families. An earthen building is an extended family, and it is also a small kingdom.

Each earthen building has its own name, most chosen from aphorisms recorded in the clan histories or to commemorate ancestors. At the same time, they express wishes for good fortune. On either side of the building's entrance is a couplet. Most of these are moral maxims containing the building's name.

Most of the earthen buildings are circular, square, or phoenix-shaped. There are also oval buildings and others shaped like the Eight Trigrams, a half moon, and an armchair. Variations exist within each shape; it can be said that there are thousands of different characteristics, but they also all share characteristics.

In the Hakka lexicon, the circular earthen buildings are called "circular stockaded villages." The term "stockaded village" can mean a village or a mountain fastness. In any case, it is a huge strategic place. Of all the shapes, the circular one is without doubt the strangest and most mysterious. Almost every circular earthen building has only one main entrance, and when it is closed, the interior is a world of its own, sheltered from everything outside. The two shutters of the entrance are thick and high, and generally covered with sheet iron; it's as if they are two armored warriors standing guard. Children stand at the sides of the door and often exert all their strength and yet they cannot budge the door. How thick is the wall of the circular building? Just imagine that it is so thick that the top of the wall can accommodate a banquet table.

14

After you enter, you see the circular building's hall. This is the passageway for going in and out of the whole building, and it is also a public lounge. Generally, long wooden benches are placed on either side of the room; when people have nothing else to do, they can sit here and chat with one another. Over time, these long wooden benches have become glossy from people sitting on them. In many halls, you see hullers for rice and other grains, stone mills, and mortars for pounding cooked glutinous rice into paste. And so you see this kind of scene: women pounding rice or milling flour, and creating sounds rich in rhythm, while the men chat about all kinds of subjects.

After you walk through the hall, there are two verandas-one along either side, as if they are two long arms gathering all of the rooms, which are of the same size and shape, into a circle. On the first floor are the kitchens, with no windows to the outside, but there are windows facing in that have a vertical wooden dividing bar. These windows are generally wide open to let in light and fresh air. Below the window, one usually finds a wooden cupboard where chickens and rabbits are raised. People may sit on top of it, so the cupboard has dual functions. The second floor functions as a storage area for food and farm tools. The bedrooms are on the third floor, and it is only beginning with the third floor that there are small strip-shaped windows.

The circular buildings have at least two staircases, and there are generally four staircases for public use. They are set up symmetrically on the two sides of the axes in the entry hall. In Pinghe and Hua'an, although the circular buildings look similar, each family has its own staircase because there is not a connecting corridor upstairs.

The courtyard has at least one well: at the side of the well, women wash vegetables and do the laundry as they chat with one another. This is another animated spot.

On the first floor of the circular buildings, in the open hall facing the entrance, is an ancestral hall for sacrificing to the ancestors' memorial tablets. Here, the clan members worship the ancestors and discuss business. If it is a relatively large circular building, sometimes there is an ancestral temple in the center of the courtyard. The temple is square, with two halls, each having rooms on both sides. It serves as both a family temple and a clan "council," and it can also serve as a school. Some circular buildings also have a smaller circular dwelling within the larger one. This creates another unusual scene inside.

Villages with circular buildings also always have square earthen buildings. The Hakka people call these earthen buildings "four-cornered buildings." Although the exterior appearance is entirely different, the interior of

the square buildings isn't much different from that of the circular ones.

The phoenix building is another popular style. It has repeated layers of random heights. It looks like a mansion or a palace, and its interior is beautifully decorated. But in the southwestern Fujian villages, they are the homes of ordinary farming families. So upon first walking into a phoenix building, few people can hide their surprise: how did it happen that in the past, mountain villages had such luxurious homes? The phoenix buildings have three halls as the core of the central axis. The left and right sides are balanced with symmetrical rooms. The number and size of these wing rooms vary according to the owner's resources. Each side may have one or two, or even three, rooms. The rooftop is gently low-pitched; the style is simple, yet impressive, distinctly resembling Han dynasty palaces. The decorations on its ridges are even more exquisite and delicate. The upturned ends on either side are shaped like ox horns or phoenix or swallow tails. The framework of the ends of the ridges is made of cast pig iron covered with lime. The ridges of the entire roof are lacquered in colors. The drawings are of peacocks, phoenixes, and other auspicious animals, birds, and plants. They look almost like the ridges of palaces. In front of the phoenix building's main entrance there is always a threshing ground, as well as a half-moon-shaped pond. The building is always lower in the front and higher in the back. The center part is high, the two sides low. Perhaps this sounds a little abstract. But if you look up at the ridge of the phoenix building, the eaves are upturned high in the air: this is exactly like a phoenix spreading its wings in preparation for flight, isn't it?

How could such mysterious and majestic rammed-earth construction emerge in this area? We need to go back in history to find the answers.

During the turmoil of the Yongjia period [304-312 A.D.], the wartime ravages of the late Tang dynasty, and the time when Jin soldiers invaded China during the Song dynasty, again and again the Hakka people's ancestors left the turbulent Central Plains and moved south. Passing through one place after another, the Hakka finally settled down in villages in southwestern Fujian where the mountains are high and the rivers long.

Those who dare to exile themselves, those who dare to take an uncertain path in fleeing for their lives, are among the best of the Han Chinese.

Amid the high mountain ranges of southwestern Fujian, the Hakka, who had experienced the vicissitudes of life, found their new home. They built wooden sheds and thatched huts. At last, they could rest and take a breath.

Like the stalwart pine seed, which can sprout and put down roots anywhere and grow into a big tree, the Hakka people were destined to be blown by the wind to a remote and backward place in a different region. They didn't complain; they were just grateful. The seed bored its way quietly from the earth and thrived in the storms; its roots spread in all directions and thrust deeply into the ground.

With a peaceful environment, fertile land, tenacious ambition, a unified spirit, and hard work, the Hakka people gradually flourished.

The Chinese people had always prayed to have many descendants. As the population of each branch of the Hakka grew rapidly, another worrisome problem surfaced: housing.

To live and work in peace and contentment: this was the simplest and most compelling desire.

Among the indelible memories of their former ancestral land was the large house surrounded by walls, but the past prosperity had vanished long ago. Day and night, they thought about how to live in peace and contentment in this place. Not only did they want the entire clan to have a secure home that would shield them from the elements, but they were even more interested in the entire clan having a home where people could live together and where their spirits would be inspired.

Now there is no way of knowing who first invented the earthen buildings. Actually, the earthen buildings weren't invented by just one person. The earthen buildings were the product of the Hakka people's passion for history, their gifted imagination, and the materials available to them. We can be sure that the first earthen building was rough and not well planned. Indeed, it might even have been laughable. But over the long years, the Hakka kept accumulating experience and making efforts to create these buildings. The rammed-earth technique became better and better, and the buildings more and more tasteful. The earthen buildings also were built higher and higher, larger and larger, more and more beautiful—like an ugly duckling that finally turns into a swan.

The Hakka came from a distant place, and also kept going to distant places. Their silhouettes on the road are portraits of the Chinese people's unceasing struggles for thousands of years. Because the several Hakka clans were constantly moving, the earthen buildings were also introduced into some counties along the southern Fujian coast.

The history of the Hakka's movement south is actually the history of part of the Han people's movement south. It was the uninterrupted movement of an entire clan. The Hakka culture gradually came to fruition and

developed during the migration and after settlement in the south.

As the crystallization of the Hakka culture, the earthen buildings did not emerge from nowhere. There were three preconditions for their coming into being: the mighty cohesive strength of a clan; a relatively peaceful living environment; and considerable financial resources.

After moving to the south from the war-torn Central Plains, the Hakka's forebears now had a tranquil place to live. After several generations of growth and development, the Hakka population rapidly increased. They also amassed quite a lot of wealth. At this time, it was finally possible for them to consider how to build a massive home where the clan members could live together.

The Hakka came from the Central Plains. Their skills in the plastic arts and their rammed-earth technique for building the earthen buildings undoubtedly also originated in the Central Plains. From the sites of primitive clan societies in Banpo, Xi'an, and Jiangjiazhai, Lintong, we can detect early forms of the earthen buildings' plastic arts. The sites of the Longshan culture and its patrilineal community at the middle and lower reaches of the Yellow River also have a large number of circular and square structures. As private ownership came into being and as the clan expanded, a kind of "Mingtang (bright hall)" structure emerged. This was the source of the Chinese traditional residence of "four lines of pillars and three rooms." It was also the basic phoenix-style structure. It's still very hard to pin down when the rammed-earth technique first appeared in China; however, in cultural sites five or six thousand years old, we can see rammed-earth platforms. The rammed-earth technique was quite well developed during the Shang dynasty [traditionally dated 1766-1122 B.C.]. The palaces of slave owners, mausoleums, ramparts, and bases for platforms were all built using rammed earth. The forts, embankments, and some buildings constructed in past dynasties all made great use of the rammed-earth technique. In the Northern Song dynasty, the rammed-earth technique made further advances. At that time, the two most authoritative monographs on construction techniques both recorded the use of rammed-earth techniques. From the time of the Ming dynasty, residences built of rammed earth could be found everywhere in China. The earthen buildings were one type of residence that reached the peak of perfection in rammed-earth technology.

Of course, in the process of being handed down, the earthen buildings' plastic arts, as well as the rammed-earth technology, changed. This happens whenever there is cultural diffusion. Anthropologists think, "Cultural

changes are a kind of adaptation based on hereditary transmission." When the Hakka constructed earthen buildings in southwestern Fujian's mountainous region, they were adapting to the natural topography of the locale.

With their thick walls and high buildings, the earthen structures were very solid and good for defense. Therefore, many people assume that they were built solely to meet defense needs. Of course, the earthen buildings had a relatively strong capacity for defense, but in fact, when the earliest earthen buildings appeared in the southwestern Fujian mountain region, it wasn't because of banditry. It was quite the opposite. Compared with the southern Fujian seaboard, the southwestern Fujian mountain region was relatively peaceful. Only because the people lived and worked in peace and contentment could they gradually amass wealth and spend years and decades ramming the costly massive earthen buildings. The southern Fujian seaboard had always suffered greatly from pirates. Beginning with the end of the Ming dynasty and the early Qing dynasty, incessant warfare occurred there. Zheng Chenggong [Koxinga, 1624-62] waged protracted warfare with the Qing army here, and countless villages were destroyed. The ordinary people became destitute and homeless, and a large number of them moved to Taiwan and Southeast Asia. In the 400 years between the early Ming Yongle period [1403-25] and the Qing Jiaqing period [1796-1820], a natural disaster-either flood or drought-occurred along the seacoast every three or four years. The ordinary people had no grain to harvest, nor did they have any way to till the land. Compared with this, the southwestern Fujian mountain region, with its high mountains, long rivers, and farming terraced fields, was much more advantageous. For defense needs, the people living along the southern Fujian coast doubtless needed earthen buildings for protection. But in fact, it was hard enough for them to subsist. How could they have constructed huge earthen buildings? Most of the earthen buildings in this area were constructed after the late Kangxi period, and most were built by the Hakka or their descendants.

As a matter of fact, the earthen buildings are good for protection; thus, perhaps the fairly recently established villages constructed earthen buildings for defense purposes. But this can't be the whole explanation. The earthen buildings couldn't have been constructed overnight. The process took a long time: if bandits attacked and now and then ransacked the village during the process, how could they have erected huge buildings?

The earthen buildings are grand and majestic. Their scale far outstrips ordinary homes in other places. The authorities in past dynasties all had specific regulations for the number of stories, number of rooms, shape of the roof, and carvings that houses could have; these were based on the owner's social status. How could the villages in southwestern Fujian have earthen buildings that clearly crossed these lines? It has been said that a woman surnamed Yu in Yongding was a favorite concubine of a Ming dynasty emperor. He gave special permission to her fellow villagers to build four or five-story mansions. But this is merely a folk tale which completely ignores the talent and enthusiasm that the Hakka ancestors had for building these structures. If it were true, the local histories certainly would have noted it. Furthermore, the earthen buildings emerged long before the Ming dynasty. The southwestern Fujian villages are remote. This area exemplifies the saying "the mountains are high, and the emperor is far away": laws couldn't reach this place, and it was difficult to enforce the government's housing regulations. During the Yuan and Qing dynasties, non-Han Chinese controlled China. This might also be a reason that the Hakka, who identified themselves as pure Han Chinese, were reluctant to submit to the laws and thus dared to cross the line.

In the earthen buildings, the Confucian and Daoist culture is epitomized in the focus on the center, the symmetry, and the feature of the front being lower and the back being higher, as well as the cohabitation of a large clan. The tangible foundation of the earthen buildings is stone; the intangible foundation is the Confucian and Daoist tradition planted in the Chinese people for hundreds of years. On top of this solid, mighty foundation is a unique world wonder.

Confucianism and Daoism aspire to the syncretism of heaven, earth, and mankind: this is the quintessence of traditional Chinese culture. This approach is manifested most brilliantly and most intensely in the earthen buildings. This is the unique irreplaceable value of the earthen buildings.

The pattern of the circular building perfectly meets the syncretism of heaven, earth, and mankind. In fengshui terminology, the courtyard in the center of the earthen building is called "the inner Taiji" or "the heavenly pond." The Hakka also often call the courtyard "the heavenly pond." Although this expression seems to be an outcome of the collective unconscious, it actually suggests that the layout of the earthen building reflects the thought of the Supreme Ultimate and yin-yang. If the Eight Trigrams pattern is used to construct the inside of a circular building, then it is an even more flawless representation of the syncretism of heaven, earth, and mankind.

The interior of the square buildings is like that of the circular buildings: it is also symmetrically arranged. The phoenix style is a little more complex, but its full layout is also circular. People generally look only at the main

building, and don't notice that in the front there is also a pond, which is half-moon-shaped, and in the rear there is the curved row of additional rooms. The pond representing yin in the front and the curved rear building representing yang make the general design of the phoenix structure a perfect circle that vividly reflects the syncretism of heaven, earth, and mankind.

Professor Mogi Keiichirou of Japan has pointed out, "The circular building is maternal; it's like the womb." The phoenix building is even more like a womb in gestation. The half-moon-shaped pond, like a womb full of water, is the yin part of the yin-yang, while the rear part of the house is the yang part symbolizing masculine vitality.

The people in the earthen buildings integrate heaven and earth, yin and yang. The heaven-earth-humanity syncretism is the realm of the highest ideals pursued by the Chinese people. The earthen building has attained this realm; combining the material and the spiritual, the earthen building represents the rich and profound meaning of China's traditional culture. The earthen building transcends a residence and thereby becomes a part of culture. In fact, the earthen building is a flourishing culture, extensive and exquisite. It is not only a type of residence, but it is also closely bound up with the lives of the Hakka people in southwestern Fujian and the other people living in southern Fujian. It is inextricably linked with them. The lives of the people living in the earthen buildings overflow with meaning, bringing warmth to the hard earthen walls. As they see it, the earthen building not only shelters them from the elements, but is also a homestead of the spirit, a spiritual symbol, and a cultural representative. As tourists see it, the earthen building is a flourishing scene of human culture.

The culture of the earthen building belongs to the people, and thus also to the world. Under the influence of globalization, it is important to preserve the distinctiveness and the integrity of the people's culture. This is a challenge for the earthen buildings. It is the people's, and it is the world's. The earthen building is a cultural legacy shared by all of the world's people. Its value will be recognized by more and more people. In the mountainous region of southwestern Fujian, the earthen building has stood for centuries. We hope that it will stand forever.

走进福建土楼——永定

永定县位于福建西部，这是一个拥有四十多万人口的闽粤边陲大县，明成化十四年（1478年）从上杭县分出置县，取名「永定」，意为「永远安定」。永定东连南靖县，东南与平和县交界，西南与广东省的大埔县、梅县接壤，西北和上杭县相连，东北与新罗区毗邻。永定是一个客家县，也是土楼分布最广、数量最多、种类最齐全的县份，学术界认为，永定是土楼的发源地。

永定土楼主要分布在湖坑、下洋、高头、抚市、高陂、岐岭等乡镇，有圆形土楼、方形土楼和府第式（又称五凤楼）土楼等，其中圆形土楼较多，而方形土楼又有诸多变异形式，如殿堂式方楼等。按照建筑结构，则几乎都是内通廊式，即各个楼层的走廊是相通的，没有阻隔。各家各户垂直拥有每层一个开间的房屋，从公共楼梯上下，生活起居显示出明显的「公共性」，这也反映了客家人注重内部团结的特征。

列入《世界遗产名录》的初溪土楼群、洪坑土楼群、高北土楼群和衍香楼、振福楼，「三群二楼」合计23座土楼，无疑是永定土楼的经典作品。其实永定土楼还有许多精制佳构的杰作值得关注，如有「天下第一农家」之称的遗经楼，由前中后三座五层方楼和左右两座四层方楼组成，是一座庞大的土楼，又是一个壮观的土楼群。又如永隆昌楼，它是两座大型方楼福盛楼和福善楼的联合体。福盛楼的门楼上刻着「大夫第」三个大字，福善楼的门楼上则是「中议第」。永隆昌并非正式楼名，而是过去土楼里经营烟丝的商号，后来约定俗成地成了楼名。永隆昌楼始建于1851至1861年间，1874年完工。两座楼连接而又各自独立，一共占地将近两万平方米，结构布局基本相似，前后左右高低错落，外围楼高四层半，正楼五层半，里面还有一些二三层的楼房。在永定土楼里，像这种官家府第式的庞然大物，多是家族兴旺，经商致富之后，耗费巨资，历经多年建成的，这和邻近的南靖土楼有所不同。如果说，永定土楼是「大宅门」，南靖土楼则大都是「小康人家」。

FUJIAN'S EARTHEN BUILDINGS

YONGDING

Yongding, a large county with a population of more than 400,000, is located in western Fujian on the border with Guangdong. Its history is one of endless turbulence. In 1478, it was carved out of Shanghang county and called "Yongding," meaning that stability would reign there forever. Yongding is bordered on the east by Nanjing county, on the southeast by Pinghe county, on the northwest by Shanghang county, on the northeast by Xinluo district, and on the southwest by Dapu and Mei counties in Guangdong. An all-Hakka county, Yongding has the most extensive, numerous, and varied earthen buildings. Academics agree that Yongding is the cradle of the earthen buildings.

Most of the Yongding earthen buildings can be found in Hukeng, Xiayang, Gaotou, Fushi, Gaobei, and Qiling. They include circular, square, and mansion-style (also called phoenix) earthen buildings. Most are circular. The square buildings have a good many variations in shape, such as the palace style. Most are constructed with an inner unobstructed connecting corridor on each floor. Each family owns a room on each floor, with each of these rooms located directly above the other. To go from one of its rooms to another, family members must take the common staircase. Thus, life in the building is more public than private. This also symbolizes the Hakka's emphasis on inner solidarity.

Now included in the World Cultural Heritage list are Yongding's Chuxi complex, Hongkeng complex, Gaobei complex, Yanxiang building, and Zhenfu building. These three complexes and two buildings comprise twenty-three earthen buildings and are undoubtedly the best of the Yongding creations. But Yongding also has many other refined and beautiful masterpieces worthy of attention. These include the Yijing building referred to as "the world's first farmhouse." It consists of five square buildings, three of them five stories and the other two four stories. It is a huge earthen building and also a spectacular complex of buildings. There is also the Yonglongchang building, which in fact comprises two large square buildings—the Fusheng and the Fushan. Yonglongchang isn't the building's formal name, but that of a tobacco business in the earthen buildings of the past; through usage, it has now become the building's name. Construction on Yonglongchang began from 1851 to 1861, and it was completed in 1874. Although the two buildings are connected and their structures are similar, each is also independent of the other. They occupy nearly 20,000 square meters of land, and are built at random heights. The outer building has four and a half floors, the main building five and a half floors, while others inside include some of two or three floors. In Yongding, most of the buildings are like the enormous residences of officials. These homes belonged to flourishing families, which—after becoming wealthy in business—expended a great amount of capital and time to build these homes. This contrasts with the earthen buildings in neighboring Nanjing county, where most of the earthen buildings are rather modest ones for ordinary people.

·23·

HISTORIC HOUSES IN FUJIAN · EARTHEN BUILDING
福建经典古民居·土楼

21 — 108

永定 YONGDING

湖坑镇洪坑村 HONGKENG VILLAGE HUKENG TOWN

❶❷❸ ZHENCHENG BUILDING
振成楼

❶ ❷

振成楼（永定）

　　位于永定县湖坑镇洪坑村，一座八卦形同圆心内外两环的土楼，占地5000平方米。外环四层高16米，184个房间；内环两层32个房间。外环以标准八卦图式分为八卦即八大单元，一卦设一部楼梯，从一层通向四层。

Zhencheng Building (Yongding)

　　It is located in Hongkeng Village, Hukeng Town, Yongding County. This earthen building with an inner and an outer ring shaped like the Eight Trigrams occupies 5000 square meters of land. The four-story outer ring is 16 meters high, and has 184 rooms; the two-story inner ring has thirty-two rooms. The outer ring is separated into eight equal sections just like the Eight Trigrams. A staircase for each section goes from the first to the fourth story.

❸

·24·

福建经典古民居·土楼
HISTORIC HOUSES
IN FUJIAN · EARTHEN
BUILDING

21 — 108

永定
YONGDING

湖坑镇洪坑村
HONGKENG VILLAGE
HUKENG TOWN

❶ 振成楼
ZHENCHENG
BUILDING

②

•25•

HISTORIC HOUSES IN FUJIAN · EARTHEN BUILDING

福建经典古民居·土楼

21—108

永定 YONGDING

湖坑镇洪坑村 HONGKENG VILLAGE HUKENG TOWN

❷❸❹❺

振成楼 ZHENCHENG BUILDING

③

④

⑤

·26·

福建经典古民居·土楼
HISTORIC HOUSES IN FUJIAN · EARTHEN BUILDING

21 — 108

永定
YONGDING

湖坑镇洪坑村
HONGKENG VILLAGE HUKENG TOWN

❶ ❷

福裕楼
FUYU BUILDING

— ❶

福裕楼（永定）

　　位于永定县湖坑镇洪坑村，1880年林氏三兄弟合资20万光洋建造的府第式方形土楼，外观像三座山，隐含三兄弟"三山"之意。整座楼在中轴线上前低后高，两座横屋，高低有序，主次分明。

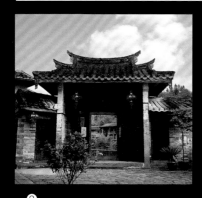

Fuyu Building (Yongding)

　　It is located in Hongkeng Village, Hukeng Town, Yongding County. In 1880, the three Lin brothers spent 200,000 silver dollars to build a mansion-style earthen building. The outer part looks like three mountains, symbolizing the three brothers. Along the central axis, the front part of the building is low and the back part high. There are wing buildings on both sides. The center is higher and the two sides lower; the layout is thoughtfully designed.

— ❷

·27·

HISTORIC HOUSES
IN FUJIAN · EARTHEN
BUILDING

福建经典古民居·土楼

21 — 108

永定
YONGDING

湖坑镇洪坑村
HONGKENG VILLAGE
HUKENG TOWN

③

福裕楼
FUYU
BUILDING

③

·28·

福建经典古民居·土楼
HISTORIC HOUSES
IN FUJIAN·EARTHEN
BUILDING

21—108

永定
YONGDING

湖坑镇洪坑村
HONGKENG VILLAGE
HUKENG TOWN

❶❷❸

福裕楼
FUYU
BUILDING

·29·

HISTORIC HOUSES IN FUJIAN · EARTHEN BUILDING

福建经典古民居·土楼

21 — 108

永定 YONGDING

湖坑镇洪坑村 HONGKENG VILLAGE HUKENG TOWN

❹❺❻

福裕楼 FUYU BUILDING

❹

❺

❻

·30·

福建经典古民居·土楼
HISTORIC HOUSES IN FUJIAN·EARTHEN BUILDING

21 — 108

永定
YONGDING

湖坑镇洪坑村
HONGKENG VILLAGE HUKENG TOWN

❶

光裕楼
GUANGYU BUILDING

❶

光裕楼（永定）

　　位于永定县湖坑镇洪坑村。建于1775年，占地面积约8000平方米。大楼为三层建筑，总计102间。楼内石门木窗精雕细刻，十分精美，是洪坑村最早、最完整的方楼。

Guangyu Building (Yongding)

　　It is located in Hongkeng Village, Hukeng Town, Yongding County. Built in 1775, Guangyu covers about 8000 sqm, It has three stories and 102 rooms in total. Magnificent and exquisite are the carvings on the stone doors and wood windows. And it is the earliest and the most intactly preserved square earth house in Hongkeng.

•31•

HISTORIC HOUSES
IN FUJIAN · EARTHEN
BUILDING

福建经典古民居·土楼

21 — 108

YONGDING
永定

HONGKENG VILLAGE
HUKENG TOWN
湖坑镇洪坑村

❷❸❹

GUANGYU
BUILDING
光裕楼

·32·

福建经典古民居·土楼
HISTORIC HOUSES IN FUJIAN·EARTHEN BUILDING

21 — 108

永定
YONGDING

湖坑镇洪坑村
HONGKENG VILLAGE HUKENG TOWN

❶❷

奎聚楼
KUIJU BUILDING

— ❶

奎聚楼（永定）

　　位于永定县湖坑镇洪坑村，占地6000平方米，始建于1834年。楼主林奎扬请翰林学士巫宜福设计。据说这是一块虎形地理，远远观之，整座楼与背后的山脊连成一体，犹如猛虎下山，奎聚楼即是"虎头"。整座方楼，宫殿般巍峨壮观。

Kuiju Building (Yongding)

　　It is located in Hongkeng Village, Hukeng Town, Yongding County. This building occupies 6000 square meters of land. Construction on it began in 1834. Its owner Lin Kuiyang engaged the Hanlin Academy scholar Wu Yifu to design it. It is said that the terrain is shaped like a tiger. Looked at from a distance, the entire building and the mountain ridge behind it seem joined together, as if a fierce tiger were rushing down the mountain. Thus, the Kuiju building is "the tiger's head." This square building is towering .

— ❷

·33·

HISTORIC HOUSES
IN FUJIAN
BUILDING
福建经典古民居·土楼

21 — 108

永定 YONGDING

湖坑镇洪坑村
HONGKENG VILLAGE
HUKENG TOWN

❸

奎聚楼
KUIJU
BUILDING

③

·34·

福建经典古民居·土楼
HISTORIC HOUSES
IN FUJIAN·EARTHEN
BUILDING

21 — 108

永定
YONGDING

湖坑镇洪坑村
HONGKENG VILLAGE
HUKENG TOWN

❶

奎聚楼
KUJU
BUILDING

HISTORIC HOUSES
IN FUJIAN · EARTHEN
BUILDING
福建经典古民居·土楼

21 — 108

永定
YONGDING

湖坑镇洪坑村
HONGKENG VILLAGE
HUKENG TOWN

①

奎聚楼
KUIJU
BUILDING

①

·36·

福建经典古民居·土楼

HISTORIC HOUSES IN FUJIAN · EARTHEN BUILDING

21 — 108

永定
YONGDING

湖坑镇洪坑村
HONGKENG VILLAGE
HUKENG TOWN

① 如升楼
RUSHENG BUILDING

①

·37·

HISTORIC HOUSES IN FUJIAN · EARTHEN BUILDING

福建经典古民居·土楼

21 — 108

永定 YONGDING

湖坑镇洪坑村 HONGKENG VILLAGE HUKENG TOWN

② 庆成楼 QINGCHENG BUILDING

③ 庆福楼 QINGFU BUILDING

④ 玉成楼 YUCHENG BUILDING

· 38 ·

福建经典古民居·土楼
HISTORIC HOUSES
IN FUJIAN · EARTHEN
BUILDING

21 — 108

永定
YONGDING

湖坑镇南溪村
NANXI VILLAGE
HUKENG TOWN

❶
振福楼
ZHENFU
BUILDING

振福楼（永定）

　　位于永定县湖坑镇南溪村。振福楼距振成楼约4000米，依山傍水，建于1913年。按八卦布局设计，占地面积4000多平方米，共有3个厅堂，96个房间。土楼内大量使用石料和砖料，雕刻精细，富丽堂皇，人们称其为振成楼的"姐妹楼"。

Zhenfu Building (Yongding)

　　It is located in Nanxi Village, Hukeng Town, Yongding County. Zhenfu building is about four kilometers from Zhencheng building. The mountain is behind it, and a river beside it. Built in 1913, it adheres to the Eight Trigrams design. It occupies more than 4000 square meters of land, and has three halls and ninety-six rooms. A lot of stone and tile was used in the interior. The carving is fine and magnificent. It is called Zhencheng's "sister building."

·39·

HISTORIC HOUSES
IN FUJIAN · EARTHEN
BUILDING
福建经典古民居 · 土楼

21—108

YONGDING
永定

NANXI VILLAGE
HUKENG TOWN
湖坑镇南溪村

❷❸

ZHENFU
BUILDING
振福楼

福建经典古民居·土楼
HISTORIC HOUSES IN FUJIAN·EARTHEN BUILDING
BUILDING

永定
YONGDING

湖坑镇南溪村
NANXI VILLAGE
HUKENG TOWN

❶
振福楼
ZHENFU
BUILDING

❶

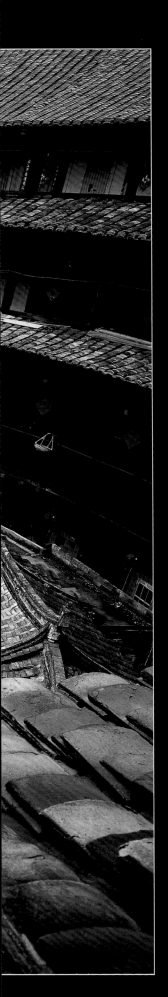

•41•

HISTORIC HOUSES
IN FUJIAN · EARTHEN
BUILDING

福建经典古民居·土楼

21—108

YONGDING
永定

NANXI VILLAGE
HUKENG TOWN
湖坑镇南溪村

ZHENFU
BUILDING
❷❸
振福楼

·42·

福建经典古民居·土楼
HISTORIC HOUSES IN FUJIAN · EARTHEN BUILDING

21—108

永定
YONGDING

湖坑镇新南村
XINNAN VILLAGE HUKENG TOWN

❶❷

衍香楼
YANXIANG BUILDING

衍香楼（永定）

　　位于永定县湖坑镇新南村。楼高四层共136间，按八卦样式构建。楼的内厅仿府第式建筑，后堂、中堂、前堂依次排列，厅左右侧有厢房。厅内及楼外围墙、左右小门装饰精美，雕刻栩栩如生，书画龙飞凤舞。楼旁一条小溪，楼后几棵古树，环境十分优美。

Yanxiang Building (Yongding)

　　It is located in Xinnan Village, Hukeng Town, Yongding County. The four-story Yanxiang building has 136 rooms, and was built in the Eight Trigrams style. The interior design is like that of mansions, with the back, center, and front halls laid out along the central axis. On the left and right sides of the halls are side rooms. The halls, the outer wall, and the doors on the left and right sides are beautifully decorated with lifelike carvings and lively, vigorous calligraphy. Next to the building is a small brook, and behind it are a few old trees: it is a lovely environment.

❶

❷

·43·

HISTORIC HOUSES
IN FUJIAN · EARTHEN
BUILDING

福建经典古民居·土楼

21 — 108

永定
YONGDING

湖坑镇新南村
XINNAN VILLAGE
HUKENG TOWN

❸

衍香楼
YANXIANG
BUILDING

福建经典古民居 · 土楼
HISTORIC HOUSES
IN FUJIAN · EARTHEN
BUILDING

21 — 108

永定
YONGDING

湖坑镇新南村
XINNAN VILLAGE
HUKENG TOWN

❶❷❸

衍香楼
YANXIANG
BUILDING

❶

❷

❸

·45·

HISTORIC HOUSES
IN FUJIAN · EARTHEN
BUILDING
福建经典古民居 · 土楼

21 — 108

永定
YONGDING

湖坑镇新南村
XINNAN VILLAGE
HUKENG TOWN

❹ ❺

衍香楼
YANXIANG
BUILDING

④

⑤

·46·

福建经典古民居·土楼
HISTORIC HOUSES IN FUJIAN · EARTHEN BUILDING

21 — 108

永定
YONGDING

湖坑镇南江村
NANJIANG VILLAGE HUKENG TOWN

❶ ❷

环极楼
HUANJI BUILDING

❶

❷

环极楼（永定）

　　位于永定县湖坑镇南江村，又称"抗震巨堡"。环极楼于1693年建成，全楼四层，高约20米，直径43.2米。第一层32开间，内环建二厅十室，主要用来接待客人。1918年2月13日永定七级地震，环极楼正面第三、四层墙体裂开一丈多长一尺多宽，震后，裂缝竟奇迹般地慢慢合拢，只留下一条细长的裂痕。

Huanji Building (Yongding)

It is located in Nanjiang Village, Hukeng Town, Yongding County. This was constructed in 1693. It is four stories and 20 meters high, and 43.2 meters in diameter. On the first floor are thirty-two rooms. The inner ring has two halls and ten rooms, most for lodging guests. When a magnitude-7 earthquake struck Yongding on February 13, 1918, the front wall of the third and fourth stories sustained a crack three meters long and one foot wide. After the earthquake, the crack miraculously came together, leaving only a long, thin scar.

·47·

HISTORIC HOUSES IN FUJIAN · EARTHEN BUILDING
福建经典古民居 · 土楼

21 — 108

YONGDING
永定

NANJIANG VILLAGE HUKENG TOWN
湖坑镇南江村

❸ ❹

HUANJI BUILDING
环极楼

❸

❹

•48•

福建经典古民居·土楼
HISTORIC HOUSES
IN FUJIAN·EARTHEN
BUILDING

21—108

永定
YONGDING

湖坑镇南溪村
NANXI VILLAGE
HUKENG TOWN

❶

南溪土楼群
NANXI'S
EARTHEN
BUILDINGS

❶

•49•

HISTORIC HOUSES IN FUJIAN · EARTHEN BUILDING
福建经典古民居·土楼

21 — 108

永定
YONGDING

湖坑镇南溪村
NANXI VILLAGE HUKENG TOWN

❶

南溪土楼群
NANXI'S EARTHEN BUILDINGS

•50•

福建经典古民居 · 土楼
HISTORIC HOUSES
IN FUJIAN · EARTHEN
BUILDING

21 — 108

永定
YONGDING

湖坑镇南溪村
NANXI VILLAGE
HUKENG TOWN

❶❷❸

南溪土楼群
NANXI'S
EARTHEN
BUILDINGS

❶

南溪土楼群（永定）

　　位于湖坑镇，包括新南、南中、南江和实佳四个自然村，顺着绵延的山势，共有大大小小土楼百余座。

Nanxi's Earthen Buildings (Yongding)

　　Nanxi is situated in Hukeng Town, including Xinnan, Nanzhong, Nanjiang and Shijia villages. You can see hundreds of earthen buildings with different sizes, stretching among the mountains.

❷

❸

HISTORIC HOUSES IN FUJIAN · EARTHEN BUILDING

福建经典古民居·土楼

21 — 108

永定 YONGDING

湖坑镇南溪村 NANXI VILLAGE HUKENG TOWN

④ 南溪土楼群 NANXI'S EARTHEN BUILDINGS

④

·52·

福建经典古民居·土楼

HISTORIC HOUSES IN FUJIAN · EARTHEN BUILDING

21 — 108

永定 YONGDING

湖坑镇南溪村 NANXI VILLAGE HUKENG TOWN

❶❷

南溪土楼群 NANXI'S EARTHEN BUILDINGS

❶

❷

•53•

HISTORIC HOUSES
IN FUJIAN · EARTHEN
BUILDING
福建经典古民居·土楼

21—108

永定
YONGDING

湖坑镇南溪村
NANXI VILLAGE
HUKENG TOWN

❸❹❺

南溪土楼群
NANXI'S
EARTHEN
BUILDINGS

·54·

福建经典古民居·土楼
HISTORIC HOUSES
IN FUJIAN · EARTHEN
BUILDING

21 — 108
永定
YONGDING

湖坑镇南溪村
NANXI VILLAGE
HUKENG TOWN

❶

做大福
THE GRAND FEAST

1

·55·

HISTORIC HOUSES IN FUJIAN · EARTHEN BUILDING

福建经典古民居·土楼

21 — 108

永定 YONGDING

湖坑镇南溪村 NANXI VILLAGE HUKENG TOWN ❶

做大福 THE GRAND FEAST

•56•

福建经典古民居·土楼
HISTORIC HOUSES
IN FUJIAN · EARTHEN
BUILDING

21 — 108

永定
YONGDING

湖坑镇南溪村
NANXI VILLAGE
HUKENG TOWN

❶❷ 做大福
THE GRAND FEAST

❶

❷

·57·

HISTORIC HOUSES IN FUJIAN · EARTHEN BUILDING

福建经典古民居·土楼

21 — 108

永定 YONGDING

湖坑镇南溪村 NANXI VILLAGE HUKENG TOWN

③

南溪土楼群 NANXI'S EARTHEN BUILDINGS

福建经典古民居·土楼

NANXI VILLAGE HUKENG TOWN

③

福建经典古民居·土楼
HISTORIC HOUSES IN FUJIAN·EARTHEN BUILDING

21—108

永定
YONGDING

湖坑镇南溪村
NANXI VILLAGE HUKENG TOWN

❶

南溪土楼群
NANXI'S EARTHEN BUILDINGS

❶

·59·

HISTORIC HOUSES
IN FUJIAN · EARTHEN
BUILDING
福建经典古民居·土楼

21 — 108

永定
YONGDING

湖坑镇南溪村
NANXI VILLAGE
HUKENG TOWN

❷

南溪土楼群
NANXI'S
EARTHEN
BUILDINGS

②

福建经典古民居·土楼
HISTORIC HOUSES
IN FUJIAN · EARTHEN
BUILDING

21 — 108

永定
YONGDING

湖坑镇南溪村
NANXI VILLAGE
HUKENG TOWN

❶

蛟塘土楼群
JIAOTANG'S
EARTHEN
BUILDINGS

❶

·61·

HISTORIC HOUSES
IN FUJIAN · EARTHEN
BUILDING

福建经典古民居 · 土楼

21 — 108

永定
YONGDING

湖坑镇南溪村
NANXI VILLAGE
HUKENG TOWN

❶

蛟塘土楼群
JIAOTANG'S
EARTHEN
BUILDINGS

·62·

福建经典古民居·土楼
HISTORIC HOUSES
IN FUJIAN · EARTHEN
BUILDING

21 — 108

永定
YONGDING

高头乡高北村
GAOBEI VILLAGE
GAOTOU TOWN

❶

承启楼
CHENGQI
BUILDING

❶

承启楼（永定）

　　位于永定县高头乡高北村，明崇祯年间破土奠基，清康熙四十八年（1709年）竣工，历经三代人。建筑占地5376平方米，直径73米，外墙周长229米。三环主楼层层叠套，外环楼四层，每层72个房间，第二环楼两层，每层40个房间，第三环为单层，有32个房间，中心一座祖堂。

Chengqi Building (Yongding)

　　This is located in Gaotou Village, Gaobei Country, Yongding County. Ground was broken for it during the Chongzhen period [1627–1644] of the Ming dynasty, but it was not until 1709three generations later—that it was finished. Occupying 5376 square meters of land, it is 73 meters in diameter. The perimeter of the outer wall is 229 meters. The main building has three rings. The four-story outer ring has seventy-two rooms on each floor. The two-story second ring has forty rooms on each floor. The third ring is a single story with thirty-two rooms. The ancestral hall is in the center.

·63·

HISTORIC HOUSES
IN FUJIAN · EARTHEN
BUILDING
福建经典古民居·土楼

21 — 108

永定
YONGDING

高头乡高北村
GAOBEI VILLAGE
GAOTOU TOWN

❷

承启楼
CHENGQI
BUILDING

•64•

福建经典古民居·土楼

HISTORIC HOUSES
IN FUJIAN·EARTHEN
BUILDING

21—108

永定
YONGDING

高头乡高北村
GAOBEI VILLAGE
GAOTOU TOWN

❶

承启楼
CHENGQI
BUILDING

1

21 — 108

永定 YONGDING

高头乡高北村 GAOBEI VILLAGE GAOTOU TOWN

❷ 承启楼 CHENGQI BUILDING

2

福建经典古民居·土楼
HISTORIC HOUSES
IN FUJIAN·EARTHEN
BUILDING

21 — 108

永定
YONGDING

高头乡高北村
GAOBEI VILLAGE
GAOTOU TOWN

❶❷❸❹

承启楼
CHENGQI
BUILDING

·67·

HISTORIC HOUSES
IN FUJIAN · EARTHEN
BUILDING

福建经典古民居·土楼

21 — 108

永定
YONGDING

高头乡高北村
GAOBEI VILLAGE
GAOTOU TOWN

承启楼
CHENGQI
BUILDING

⑤

①

•69•

HISTORIC HOUSES IN FUJIAN · EARTHEN BUILDING

福建经典古民居 · 土楼

21 — 108

永定 YONGDING

高头乡高北村 GAOBEI VILLAGE GAOTOU TOWN

❷ 世泽楼 SHIZE BUILDING

2

福建经典古民居·土楼
HISTORIC HOUSES
IN FUJIAN
BUILDING · EARTHEN

21 — 108

永定
YONGDING

高头乡高北村
GAOBEI VILLAGE
GAOTOU TOWN

❶

五云楼
WUYUN
BUILDING

❶

·71·

HISTORIC HOUSES IN FUJIAN · EARTHEN BUILDING
福建经典古民居 · 土楼
21—108

永定 YONGDING

高头乡高北村 GAOBEI VILLAGE GAOTOU TOWN
❷❸

五云楼 WUYUN BUILDING

侨福楼 QIAOFU BUILDING
❹

·72·

福建经典古民居·土楼

HISTORIC HOUSES IN FUJIAN·EARTHEN BUILDING

21 — 108

永定

YONGDING

大溪乡

DAXI TOWN

❶

大溪土楼群

DAXI'S EARTHEN BUILDINGS

❶

HISTORIC HOUSES IN FUJIAN · EARTHEN BUILDING

福建经典古民居·土楼

21—108

YONGDING 永定

DAXI TOWN 大溪乡

❷❸

DAXI'S EARTHEN BUILDINGS 大溪土楼群

·74·

福建经典古民居·土楼
HISTORIC HOUSES
IN FUJIAN·EARTHEN
BUILDING

21 — 108

永定
YONGDING

大溪乡坑头村
KENGTOU VILLAGE
DAXI TOWN

❶❷

善庆楼
SHANQING
BUILDING

①

②

·75·

福建经典古民居·土楼
HISTORIC HOUSES
IN FUJIAN · EARTHEN
BUILDING

21 — 108

永定
YONGDING

大溪乡坑头村
KENGTOU VILLAGE
DAXI TOWN
③

田心楼
TIANXIN
BUILDING
④

崇裕楼
CHONGYU
BUILDING
⑤ ⑥

福和楼
FUHE
BUILDING

福建经典古民居·土楼
HISTORIC HOUSES
IN FUJIAN·EARTHEN
BUILDING

21—108

永定
YONGDING

大溪乡
DAXI TOWN

❶ ❷ ❸
东华楼
DONGHUA
BUILDING

❹ ❺
镇江楼
ZHENJIANG
BUILDING

❻
世昌楼
SHICHANG
BUILDING

·77·

HISTORIC HOUSES
IN FUJIAN · EARTHEN
BUILDING

福建经典古民居·土楼

21 — 108

永定 YONGDING

大溪乡 DAXI TOWN

⑦

太和楼 TAIHE BUILDING

⑧

复兴楼 FUXING BUILDING

⑨⑩⑪

大溪土楼 DAXI'S EARTHEN BUILDINGS

· 78 ·

福建经典古民居 · 土楼
HISTORIC HOUSES
IN FUJIAN · EARTHEN
BUILDING

21 — 108

永定
YONGDING

陈东乡岩太村
YANTAI VILLAGE
CHENDONG TOWN
❶

岩太土楼群
YANTAI'S
EARTHEN
BUILDINGS

❶

·79·

HISTORIC HOUSES
IN FUJIAN · EARTHEN
BUILDING

福建经典古民居·土楼

21 — 108

永定 YONGDING

陈东乡岩太村 YANTAI VILLAGE
CHENDONG TOWN

❷

岩太土楼群 YANTAI'S
EARTHEN
BUILDINGS

·80·

福建经典古民居·土楼
HISTORIC HOUSES
IN FUJIAN · EARTHEN
BUILDING

21—108
YONGDING

陈东乡岩太村
YANTAI VILLAGE
CHENDONG TOWN

❶❷

岩太土楼群
YANTAI'S
EARTHEN
BUILDINGS

·81·

HISTORIC HOUSES
IN FUJIAN · EARTHEN
BUILDING
福建经典古民居·土楼

21 — 108

永定
YONGDING

古竹乡
GUZHU TOWN

❸

古竹土楼群
GUZHU'S
EARTHEN
BUILDINGS

❸

·82·

福建经典古民居·土楼
HISTORIC HOUSES IN FUJIAN · EARTHEN BUILDING

21 — 108

永定
YONGDING

高陂镇上洋村
SHANGYANG VILLAGE GAOPI TOWN

❶❷❸

遗经楼
YIJING BUILDING

❶ ————— ❷

遗经楼（永定）

　　位于永定县高陂镇上洋村，有"天下第一农家"之称。由前中后三座五层方楼和左右两座四层方楼组成，东西宽136米，南北长76米，主楼高17米，共占地面积10336平方米，房间400间、厅24个。据说从清嘉庆十一年（1806年）开始动工兴建，经过三代人，整整用了70年才建成。

Yijing Building (Yongding)

　　Located in Shangyang Village, Gaopi town,Yongding County, it is called "The World's First Farmhouse." It comprises three five-story square buildings in the front, center, and back, and two four-story square buildings on the left and right. It is either one huge earthen building or a spectacular group of earthen buildings. It is 136 meters wide, east to west, and 76 meters long, north to south. The main building is 17 meters high, and occupies 10,336 square meters of land. There are 400 rooms and twenty-four halls. It is said that it took seventy years to build, with construction beginning in 1806 and lasting three generations.

❸

HISTORIC HOUSES
IN FUJIAN · EARTHEN
BUILDING
福建经典古民居·土楼

21—108

永定
YONGDING

高陂镇上洋村
SHANGYANG VILLAGE
GAOPI TOWN

❹

遗经楼
YIJING
BUILDING

•84•

福建经典古民居·土楼
HISTORIC HOUSES
IN FUJIAN · EARTHEN
BUILDING

21 — 108

永定
YONGDING

高陂镇上洋村
SHANGYANG VILLAGE
GAOPI TOWN

❶ 遗经楼
YIJING
BUILDING

·85·

HISTORIC HOUSES IN FUJIAN · EARTHEN BUILDING

福建经典古民居·土楼

21—108

永定

YONGDING

高陂镇上洋村

SHANGYANG VILLAGE GAOPI TOWN

❶

遗经楼

YIJING BUILDING

福建经典古民居·土楼
HISTORIC HOUSES
IN FUJIAN · EARTHEN
BUILDING

21 — 108

永定
YONGDING

高陂镇上洋村
SHANGYANG VILLAGE
GAOPI TOWN

❶ ❷ ❸

遗经楼
YIJING
BUILDING

❶

❷

❸

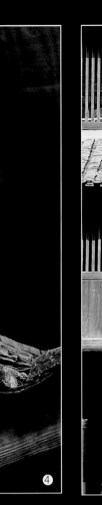

·87·

HISTORIC HOUSES IN FUJIAN · EARTHEN BUILDING

福建经典古民居·土楼

21 — 108

永定 YONGDING

高陂镇上洋村 SHANGYANG VILLAGE GAOPI TOWN

④⑤⑥⑦

遗经楼 YIJING BUILDING

·88·

福建经典古民居·土楼
HISTORIC HOUSES IN FUJIAN · EARTHEN BUILDING

21 — 108

永定
YONGDING

高陂镇富岭村
FULING VILLAGE GAOPI TOWN

❶ ❷

裕隆楼（五凤楼）
YULONG BUILDINGS

❶

裕隆楼（永定）

位于永定县高陂镇富岭村大塘角。清道光八年(1828年)动工历时6年建成。主体建筑坐南朝北，对称布局,面宽52米，进深53米，分左中右三部分。后高前低，呈五凤形状。整个建筑群布局规整，古朴庄重。

Yulong Building (Yongding)

Located in Fuling Village, Gaopi Town, Yongding County, this building began its construction in the 8th year of the Daoguang Emperor's reign, Qing Dynasty and was completed 6 years later. Facing south, 52 meters wide, 53 meters deep, this hakka house has 3 compounds and was symmetrically designed. Lower in the front and higher in the rear, this five-phoenix shape castle was regularly laid out, simple, unsophisticated and grave.

❷

HISTORIC HOUSES
IN FUJIAN · EARTHEN
BUILDING
福建经典古民居 · 土楼
21 — 108

YONGDING
永定

FULING VILLAGE
GAOPI TOWN
高陂镇富岭村

❸❹❺❻

YULONG
BUILDING
裕隆楼（五凤楼）

3

4

5

6

·90·

福建经典古民居·土楼
HISTORIC HOUSES IN FUJIAN · EARTHEN BUILDING

21—108

永定
YONGDING

湖雷镇下寨村
XIAZHAI VILLAGE HULEI TOWN

❶❷

馥馨楼
FUXIN BUILDING

馥馨楼（永定）

位于永定县湖雷镇下寨村。据楼内居民保存的孔氏族谱记载，楼建于唐代宗大历四年（769年），是闽西南现存最古老的土楼。馥馨楼没有石基，沿袭中原先祖的建筑技术和建筑形式，墙体全部以土夯成，墙厚1.3米，高三层，内部格局与通常方楼不同，上下两堂式，楼门厅即下堂敞厅，前面相对的是中堂敞厅。现损坏较为严重。

Fuxin Building (Yongding)

This building is located next to the main road in Xiazhai Village, Hulei Town.Yongding County, According to the Kong clan genealogy, it was built in 769: it is the oldest earthen building extant in southwestern Fujian. The Fuxin building doesn't have a stone foundation. In accord with the construction techniques and style of the Hakka people's ancestors on the Central Plains, the wall was made of rammed earth and is 1.3 meters thick and three stories tall. Its interior is different from the usual square buildings: there are two halls. When you walk in, you come to the open lower hall; facing it, the open central hall lies ahead. The building has sustained quite a lot of damage.

•91•

HISTORIC HOUSES IN FUJIAN · EARTHEN BUILDING

福建经典古民居 · 土楼

21—108

永定 YONGDING

湖雷镇下寨村 XIAZHAI VILLAGE HULEI TOWN

❸❹❺

馥馨楼 FUXIN BUILDING

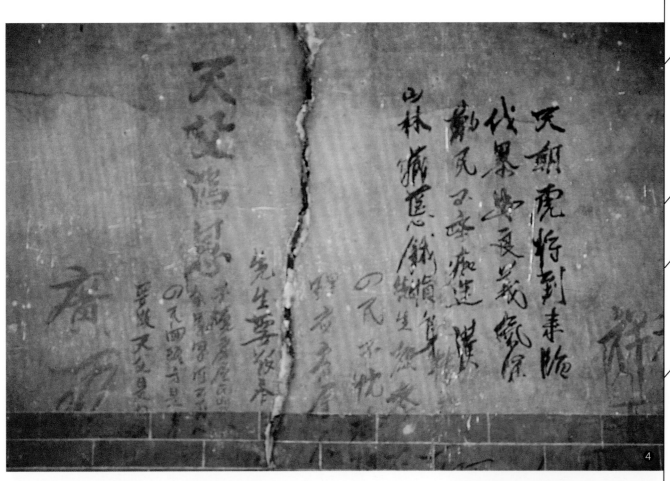

福建经典古民居·土楼
HISTORIC HOUSES IN FUJIAN·EARTHEN BUILDING

21 — 108

永定
YONGDING

湖雷镇湖瑶村
HUYAO VILLAGE HULEI TOWN

❶
火烧楼
HUOSHAO (FIRE-BURNT) BUILDING

火烧楼（永定）

　　位于永定县湖雷镇湖瑶村，相传太平天国时期被烧毁，现仅存几堵断墙，原名已佚，当地人称之为火烧楼。

Huoshao (Fire-burnt) Building (Yongding)

　　Located in the Huyao Village, Hulei Town, Yongding County, this building was burnt down during the Taiping Heavenly Kingdom (1851-1864). With its original name unknown and several worn-out walls remained, this building is called the Huoshao(Fire-burnt) Building by the locals.

·93·

HISTORIC HOUSES
IN FUJIAN · EARTHEN
BUILDING

福建经典古民居·土楼

21 — 108

永定 YONGDING

湖雷镇湖瑶村 HUYAO VILLAGE
HULEI TOWN

②

火烧楼 HUOSHAO
(FIRE-BURNT)
BUILDING

②

·94·

福建经典古民居·土楼
HISTORIC HOUSES
IN FUJIAN·EARTHEN
BUILDING

21—108

永定
YONGDING

抚市镇
FUSHI TOWN

❶

抚市土楼群
FUSHI'S
EARTHEN
BUILDINGS

·95·

HISTORIC HOUSES
IN FUJIAN · EARTHEN
BUILDING

福建经典古民居·土楼

21—108

永定 YONGDING

抚市镇 FUSHI TOWN

②③
④⑤⑥

抚市土楼群 FUSHI'S EARTHEN BUILDINGS

·96·

福建经典古民居·土楼
HISTORIC HOUSES IN FUJIAN · EARTHEN BUILDING

21 — 108

永定
YONGDING

抚市镇新民村
XINMIN VILLAGE FUSHI TOWN

五福楼
WUFU BUILDING

❶ ❷
❸ ❹ ❺

❶

❷

❸

❹

❺

·97·

HISTORIC HOUSES IN FUJIAN · EARTHEN BUILDING

福建经典古民居·土楼

21—108

YONGDING 永定

XINMIN VILLAGE FUSHI TOWN 抚市镇新民村

❻❼

FUXIN BUILDING 福新楼

福建经典古民居·土楼
HISTORIC HOUSES IN FUJIAN·EARTHEN BUILDING

·98·

21 — 108

永定
YONGDING

抚市镇新民村
XINMIN VILLAGE
FUSHI TOWN

❶❷

永隆昌楼
YONGLONGCHANG
BUILDING

❶

永隆昌楼（永定）

　　位于永定县抚市镇新民村。永隆昌并非楼名，而是旧时楼里经营烟丝的商号，相沿成习，称其为永隆昌楼。它由两座大型方楼福盛楼和福善楼组成，福盛楼门楼刻"大夫第"三个大字，福善楼门楼则刻"中议第"。始建于1851至1861年间，1874年完工。两座楼既独立又连接，共占地近两万平方米，结构布局基本相似，前后左右高低错落。

❷

Yonglongchang Building (Yongding)

　　Located in Xinmin Village, Fushi Town, Yongding County, Yonglongchang isn't the structure's formal name, but is the name of a tobacco firm whose business was in this building. Yonglongchang is actually a combination of two large buildings, the Fusheng building and the Fushan building. Carved on the arch of the Fusheng building are three large characters, "Dafu's Residence." On the arch of the Fushan building is written "Zhongyi Residence." Construction began in 1851–1861 and was completed in 1874. The two buildings are both independent and linked. Together, they occupy nearly 20000 square meters of land, and have essentially the same design. The front, back, and two sides differ in their heights.

·99·

HISTORIC HOUSES IN FUJIAN · EARTHEN BUILDING
福建经典古民居·土楼

21 — 108

永定 YONGDING

抚市镇新民村 XINMIN VILLAGE FUSHI TOWN

❸❹

永隆昌楼 YONGLONGCHANG BUILDING

❸

❹

·100·

福建经典古民居·土楼
HISTORIC HOUSES IN FUJIAN · EARTHEN BUILDING

21 — 108
永定
YONGDING

抚市镇新民村
XINMIN VILLAGE
FUSHI TOWN

①②③④

永隆昌楼
YONGLONGCHANG
BUILDING

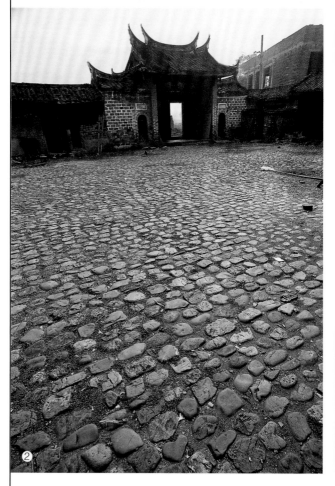

•101•

HISTORIC HOUSES IN FUJIAN · EARTHEN BUILDING

福建经典古民居 · 土楼

21 — 108

永定 YONGDING

抚市镇新民村 XINMIN VILLAGE FUSHI TOWN

⑤⑥⑦⑧⑨

永隆昌楼 YONGLONGCHANG BUILDING

福建经典古民居·土楼
HISTORIC HOUSES
IN FUJIAN · EARTHEN
BUILDING

21 — 108

永定
YONGDING

下洋镇初溪村
CHUXI VILLAGE
XIAYANG TOWN

❶

初溪土楼群
CHUXI'S
EARTHEN
BUILDINGS

❶

初溪土楼群（永定）

　　位于永定县下洋镇初溪村。五座圆楼和数十座方楼高低错落散布在开阔的盆地上，一条鹅卵石小道像纽带一样连接每座土楼，背后青山密林，山坡上梯田层层叠叠。集庆楼是初溪现存最古老的一座圆楼，为徐氏三世祖于明永乐十七年(1419年)兴建。

Chuxi's Earthen Buildings (Yongding)

　　They are located in Chuxi Village, Xiayang Town, Yongding County. The five circular buildings and several dozen square buildings are scattered randomly over the wide basin. A small path made of cobblestones links these earthen buildings. Behind the buildings are terraced hills and dense forests. The oldest circular building among the extant Chuxi structures is Jiqing, built by the third generation of the Xu clan in 1419.

·103·

HISTORIC HOUSES
IN FUJIAN · EARTHEN
BUILDING

福建经典古民居·土楼

21—108

YONGDING

永定

CHUXI VILLAGE
XIAYANG TOWN

下洋镇初溪村

❷

CHUXI'S
EARTHEN
BUILDINGS

初溪土楼群

福建经典古民居·土楼

HISTORIC HOUSES
IN FUJIAN·EARTHEN
BUILDING

21 — 108

永定
YONGDING

下洋镇初溪村
CHUXI VILLAGE
XIAYANG TOWN

❶

初溪土楼群
CHUXI'S
EARTHEN
BUILDINGS

❶

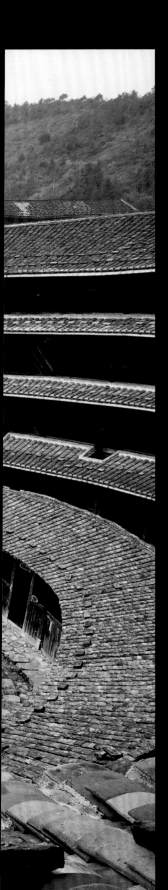

•105•

HISTORIC HOUSES
IN FUJIAN · EARTHEN
BUILDING

福建经典古民居 · 土楼

21 — 108

永定
YONGDING

下洋镇初溪村
CHUXI VILLAGE
XIAYANG TOWN

②

初溪土楼群
CHUXI'S
EARTHEN
BUILDINGS

福建经典古民居 · 土楼

HISTORIC HOUSES
IN FUJIAN · EARTHEN
BUILDING

21 — 108

永定
YONGDING

下洋镇初溪村
CHUXI VILLAGE
XIAYANG TOWN

❶ ❷ ❸

初溪土楼群
CHUXI'S
EARTHEN
BUILDINGS

❶

❷

❸

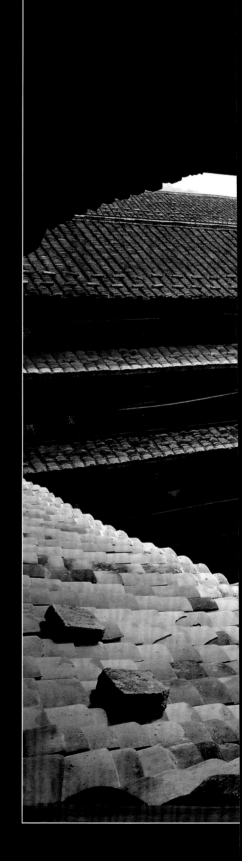

•107•

福建经典古民居·土楼

HISTORIC HOUSES
IN FUJIAN · EARTHEN
BUILDING

21—108

永定 YONGDING

下洋镇初溪村 CHUXI VILLAGE
XIAYANG TOWN

❹

初溪土楼群 CHUXI'S
EARTHEN
BUILDINGS

·108·

福建经典古民居·土楼
HISTORIC HOUSES
IN FUJIAN · EARTHEN
BUILDING

21 — 108

永定
YONGDING

下洋镇初溪村
CHUXI VILLAGE
XIAYANG TOWN

①

初溪土楼群
CHUXI'S
EARTHEN
BUILDINGS

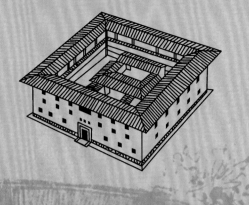

走进福建土楼 —— 南靖

南靖县古称兰水县，南者即地处福建之南，靖者取安靖之义，建县于元至正十六年（1356年），居民主体为闽南人，与永定县交界的书洋、梅林两镇则多为客家人。南靖土楼主要分布在这两个乡镇，船场、南坑、和溪、奎洋等乡镇也有少量土楼。

南靖土楼除了数量上略少于永定，在种类上、形态上并不逊色。

许多土楼依山而筑，错落有致，构成村落，蔚为壮观。如书洋镇的塔下村，清澈闪亮的溪水，像银链一样把山脚下、溪岸边二十多座形态各异的土楼，串成一个美妙绝伦的村寨，溪水从土楼门前流淌而过，给古老的土楼群平添了一份生机。又如书洋镇的石桥村，长源楼建于临溪的陡峭坡地上，远看像一条横卧的长龙，前低后高起伏很大，全村几十座土楼都依山傍水，巍峨耸立。再如书洋镇的南欧村，梅林镇的梅林村、长教村等，都是土楼与自然环境完美融合的村落。这些地方的土楼虽然没有田螺坑土楼群的名气，却也可圈可点，它们的建筑艺术和审美价值正在被越来越多的人所认识。

南靖土楼之中的歪歪斜斜裕昌楼、袖珍型土楼翠林楼，也拥有其独特奇异之妙。

FUJIAN'S EARTHEN BUILDINGS

NANJING

In ancient times, Nanjing county was called Lanshui county. "Nan" refers to its southern location in Fujian and "jing" means peaceful. The county was established in 1356. Most of its residents are from southern Fujian, except for those in Shuyang and Meilin towns, both bordering Yongding, who are Hakka. Most of Nanjing's earthen buildings are located in these two towns, while there are also a few earthen buildings in the villages and towns of Chuanchang, Nankeng, Hexi, and Kuiyang.

Although there are fewer earthen buildings in Nanjing than in Yongding, they are just as impressive in their styles. Several, built against mountains and forming villages, are spectacular. For example: In Taxia village in Shuyang, the limpid, glistening brook is like a silver chain connecting the more than twenty earthen buildings in the foothills into a lovely village. The brook runs through the entire village, flowing past the ancient earthen buildings and enhancing their vitality. In Shiqiao village in Shuyang, the Changyuan building was constructed on a craggy slope facing the brook. From a distance, it looks like a sleeping dragon. Several dozen earthen buildings in the village tower against mountains and water. Nan'ou village in Shuyang, Meilin village and Changjiao village in Meilin town all integrate the environment with the earthen buildings. Although the earthen buildings in these places are not as well known as the Tianluokeng complex of earthen buildings, they are still remarkable. Their construction skill and their value are being increasingly recognized.

The most unusual earthen buildings in Nanjing are the tilted Yuchang building and the tiny Cuilin building. You mustn't miss seeing them.

·111·

HISTORIC HOUSES IN FUJIAN · EARTHEN BUILDING
福建经典古民居·土楼

109 — 174

南靖 NANJING

书洋镇上坂村 SHANGBAN VILLAGE SHUYANG TOWN

❶ 江夏堂 JIANGXIA BUILDING

❷ 田螺坑土楼群 TIANLUOKENG'S EARTHEN BUILDINGS

田螺坑土楼群（南靖）

　　位于南靖县书洋镇上坂村。由四座圆楼和一座方楼组成，气势非凡。一方四圆，如四个圆环围着一个方框，又如一个方框系着四个圆环，错落有致，疏密得体。

Tianluokeng's Earthen Buildings (Nanjing)

　　These are located in Shangban Village, Shuyang Town, Nanjing County. The complex comprises four circular buildings and one square one. They are extraordinary—like four circular rings enclosing one square, or like one square tying four circular rings together. The placement is precise and tasteful.

·112·

福建经典古民居·土楼
HISTORIC HOUSES
IN FUJIAN·EARTHEN
BUILDING

109—174

南靖
NANJING

书洋镇上坂村
SHANGBAN VILLAGE
SHUYANG TOWN

❶ 田螺坑土楼群
TIANLUOKENG'S
EARTHEN
BUILDINGS

• 113 •

HISTORIC HOUSES
IN FUJIAN · EARTHEN
BUILDING
NANJING

福建经典古民居·土楼

南靖

109 — 174

SHANGBAN VILLAGE
SHUYANG TOWN

书洋镇上坂村

❶

TIANLUOKENG'S
EARTHEN
BUILDINGS

田螺坑土楼群

·114·

福建经典古民居·土楼
HISTORIC HOUSES
IN FUJIAN · EARTHEN
BUILDING

109 — 174

南靖
NANJING

书洋镇上坂村
SHANGBAN VILLAGE
SHUYANG TOWN

❶❷❸❹

振昌楼
ZHENCHANG
BUILDING

❶

❷

❸

❹

·115·

HISTORIC HOUSES IN FUJIAN · EARTHEN BUILDING

福建经典古民居·土楼

109 — 174

南靖 NANJING

书洋镇上坂村 SHANGBAN VILLAGE SHUYANG TOWN

⑤⑥⑦⑧

和昌楼 HECHANG BUILDING

⑤

福建经典古民居·土楼
HISTORIC HOUSES
IN FUJIAN·EARTHEN
BUILDING

109 — 174

南靖
NANJING

书洋镇上坂村
SHANGBAN VILLAGE
SHUYANG TOWN

❶❷❸

步云楼
BUYUN
BUILDING

•117•

福建经典古民居·土楼

HISTORIC HOUSES
IN FUJIAN · EARTHEN
BUILDING
BUILDING

109 — 174

南靖 NANJING

书洋镇上坂村 SHANGBAN VILLAGE
SHUYANG TOWN

瑞云楼 RUIYUN
BUILDING
④⑤

·118·

福建经典古民居·土楼
HISTORIC HOUSES IN FUJIAN·EARTHEN BUILDING

109 — 174

南靖
NANJING

书洋镇上坂村
SHANGBAN VILLAGE SHUYANG TOWN

①②③④

文昌楼
WENCHANG BUILDING

·119·

HISTORIC HOUSES IN FUJIAN · EARTHEN BUILDING
福建经典古民居·土楼

109 — 174

NANJING
南靖

SHANGBAN VILLAGE SHUYANG TOWN
书洋镇上坂村

⑤⑥⑦

TIANLUOKENG'S EARTHEN EARTHEN BUILDINGS
田螺坑土楼群

·120·

福建经典古民居·土楼
HISTORIC HOUSES
IN FUJIAN·EARTHEN
BUILDING

109 — 174

南靖
NANJING

书洋镇上坂村
SHANGBAN VILLAGE
SHUYANG TOWN

❶ ❷ ❸

田螺坑夜景
TIANLUOKENG'S
EARTHEN
BUILDINGS

·121·

HISTORIC HOUSES IN FUJIAN · EARTHEN BUILDING

福建经典古民居·土楼

109 — 174

南靖 NANJING

书洋镇上坂村 SHANGBAN VILLAGE SHUYANG TOWN

❹❺❻

田螺坑夜景 TIANLUOKENG'S EARTHEN EARTHEN BUILDINGS

福建经典古民居·土楼
HISTORIC HOUSES IN FUJIAN·EARTHEN BUILDING

109 — 174

南靖
NANJING

书洋镇下坂村
XIABAN VILLAGE SHUYANG TOWN

❶ ❷

裕昌楼
YUCHANG BUILDING

裕昌楼（南靖）

位于南靖县书洋镇下坂村，又叫东倒西歪楼、歪歪斜斜楼。外观上看不出来，当你一脚踏进楼门，就会看到全楼回廊的支柱左倾右斜，最大的倾角达到15度。裕昌楼始建于元朝中期（1308–1338年间），为刘、罗、张、唐、范五姓合建，高五层，每层54个房间。全楼分成五大单元，每一单元有一部楼梯，五个家族各居一个单元，现仅住刘姓十几户人家。

Yuchang Building (Nanjing)

Located in Xiaban Village, Shuyang Town, Nanjing County, it is also called the tilted building. You can't see this from the outside, but as soon as you step into the building, you can see that the supporting pillars in the whole corridor slant either to the left or right; the greatest slant is at a 15-degree angle. Construction on Yuchang began between 1308 and 1338; it was built by the Liu, Luo, Zhang, Tang, and Fan clans. Each of the five stories has fifty-four rooms, and the whole building is divided into five units with a staircase for each. The five clans each lived in one section; now it is only ten or more households of the Liu clan who live there.

·123·

HISTORIC HOUSES
IN FUJIAN · EARTHEN
BUILDING

福建经典古民居 · 土楼

109 — 174

NANJING
南靖

XIABAN VILLAGE
SHUYANG TOWN
书洋镇下坂村

❸

YUCHANG
BUILDING
裕昌楼

❸

·124·

福建经典古民居·土楼
HISTORIC HOUSES
IN FUJIAN · EARTHEN
BUILDING

109 — 174

南靖
NANJING

书洋镇下坂村
XIABAN VILLAGE
SHUYANG TOWN

❶

下坂土楼群
XIABAN'S
EARTHEN
BUILDINGS

·125·

HISTORIC HOUSES IN FUJIAN · EARTHEN BUILDING

福建经典古民居·土楼

109 — 174

南靖 NANJING

书洋镇下坂村 XIABAN VILLAGE SHUYANG TOWN

❶

下坂土楼群 XIABAN'S EARTHEN BUILDINGS

·126·

福建经典古民居·土楼
HISTORIC HOUSES
IN FUJIAN · EARTHEN
BUILDING

109 — 174

南靖
NANJING

书洋镇典江村
DIANJIANG VILLAGE
SHUYANG TOWN

❶

河坑土楼群
HEKENG'S
EARTHEN
BUILDINGS

❶

·127·

HISTORIC HOUSES
IN FUJIAN · EARTHEN
BUILDING

福建经典古民居·土楼

109 — 174

南靖
NANJING

书洋镇典江村
DIANJIANG VILLAGE
SHUYANG TOWN

❶

河坑土楼群
HEKENG'S
EARTHEN
BUILDINGS

福建经典古民居·土楼

HISTORIC HOUSES
IN FUJIAN · EARTHEN
BUILDING

109 — 174

南靖
NANJING

书洋镇典江村
DIANJIANG VILLAGE
SHUYANG TOWN

❶
春贵楼（外景）
CHUNGUI
BUILDING

❷
东升楼（外景）
DONGSHENG
BUILDING

❸
晓春楼（外景）
XIAOCHUN
BUILDING

①

②

③

HISTORIC HOUSES IN FUJIAN · EARTHEN BUILDING

福建经典古民居·土楼

109 — 174

NANJING 南靖

DIANJIANG VILLAGE SHUYANG TOWN 书洋镇典江村

❹ CHUNGUI BUILDING 春贵楼（内景）

❺ DONGSHENG BUILDING 东升楼（内景）

❻ XIAOCHUN BUILDING 晓春楼（内景）

❹

福建经典古民居·土楼
HISTORIC HOUSES IN FUJIAN · EARTHEN BUILDING

109 — 174

南靖
NANJING

书洋镇典江村
DIANJIANG VILLAGE SHUYANG TOWN

❶

河远土楼群
HEYUAN'S EARTHEN BUILDINGS

❶

·131·

HISTORIC HOUSES
IN FUJIAN · EARTHEN
BUILDING
福建经典古民居·土楼

109 — 174

NANJING
南靖

DIANJIANG VILLAGE
SHUYANG TOWN
书洋镇典江村

HEYUAN'S
EARTHEN
BUILDINGS
河远土楼群
❷

❷

·132·

福建经典古民居·土楼
HISTORIC HOUSES IN FUJIAN·EARTHEN BUILDING

109 — 174

南靖
NANJING

书洋镇石桥村
SHIQIAO VILLAGE SHUYANG TOWN

❶

长源楼
CHANGYUAN BUILDING

❶

长源楼（南靖）

　　位于南靖县书洋镇石桥村。建于清雍正元年（1723年），沿溪边用鹅卵石垒起一道6米多高的溪坎，长源楼的外墙就建在这道溪坎上。主楼三层，一楼是四方形敞廊，二楼、三楼有凹字形三边走廊。建筑学家称之为"斜面土楼"，当地人则叫它"交椅楼"。

Changyuan Building (Nanjing)

　　Located in Shiqiao Village, Shuyang Town, NanJing County, this was built in 1723. The out wall of Changyuan Building was constructed on a six-meter-high river embankment built with cobblestones. The main building has three stories. The first floor has an open square veranda; the second and third floors have verandas shaped like the character "凹". Architects call it "obliqueplane," while the locals call it an "armchair building."

•133•

HISTORIC HOUSES
IN FUJIAN · EARTHEN
BUILDING

福建经典古民居·土楼

109 — 174

南靖
NANJING

书洋镇石桥村
SHIQIAO VILLAGE
SHUYANG TOWN

❷

长源楼
CHANGYUAN
BUILDING

福建经典古民居·土楼
HISTORIC HOUSES
IN FUJIAN·EARTHEN
BUILDING

109 — 174

南靖
NANJING

书洋镇石桥村
SHIQIAO VILLAGE
SHUYANG TOWN

❶

长源楼
CHANGYUAN
BUILDING

❶

·135·

HISTORIC HOUSES
IN FUJIAN · EARTHEN
BUILDING
福建经典古民居·土楼

109 — 174
NANJING
南靖

SHIQIAO VILLAGE
SHUYANG TOWN
书洋镇石桥村

❷❸❹
CHANGYUAN
BUILDING
长源楼

福建经典古民居·土楼
HISTORIC HOUSES IN FUJIAN·EARTHEN BUILDING

109 — 174

南靖
NANJING

书洋镇石桥村
SHIQIAO VILLAGE SHUYANG TOWN

❶❷
❸❹❺

顺裕楼
SHUNYU BUILDING

①

②

④

⑤

③

顺裕楼（南靖）

　　位于南靖县书洋镇石桥村，为单环式圆楼，直径74.1米，建于1943年，虽然年代比较迟，但它的单环敞廊式样却是圆楼古老的标准造型，显出一种复古的意味。

Shunyu Building (Nanjing)

　　It is located in Shiqiao Village, Shuyang Town,Nanjing County. This building is a single circle round earthen house, 74.1 meters in diameter, built in 1943. Though it hasn't got a long history, its single ring with open corridor structure is the standard structure of old building with a taste of returning to the old age.

·137·

HISTORIC HOUSES IN FUJIAN · EARTHEN BUILDING
福建经典古民居·土楼

109 — 174

NANJING
南靖

SHIQIAO VILLAGE SHUYANG TOWN
书洋镇石桥村

❻❼❽

HANWEI BUILDING
捍卫楼

❻

❼

❽

·138·

福建经典古民居·土楼
HISTORIC HOUSES IN FUJIAN · EARTHEN BUILDING

109 — 174

南靖
NANJING

书洋镇五更寮村
WUGENGLIAO VILLAGE SHUYANG TOWN

❶ ❷ ❸

五更寮土楼群
WUGENGLIAO'S EARTHEN BUILDINGS

❶

❷

❸

五更寮土楼群（南靖）

　　位于南靖县书洋镇五更寮村，10余座圆形土楼虽名不见经传，更显得朴实本色。

Wugengliao's earthen buildings (Nanjing)

　　It is located in Wugengliao Village, Shuyang Town, Nanjing County. It has over ten buildings, not well known, yet exhibits their plain nature.

·139·

HISTORIC HOUSES IN FUJIAN · EARTHEN BUILDING

福建经典古民居·土楼

109—174

NANJING

南靖

WUGENGLIAO VILLAGE SHUYANG TOWN

书洋镇五更寮村

❹❺❻

WUGENGLIAO'S EARTHEN BUILDINGS

五更寮土楼群

·140·

福建经典古民居·土楼
HISTORIC HOUSES IN FUJIAN · EARTHEN BUILDING
BUILDING

109 — 174

南靖
NANJING

书洋镇田中村
TIANZHONG VILLAGE SHUYANG TOWN

❶

龙潭楼
LONGTAN BUILDING

龙潭楼（南靖）

　　位于南靖县书洋镇田中村，方形土楼，已有300年历史，其后裔子孙多迁居台湾。

Longtan Building (Nanjing)

　　It is located in Tianzhong Village, Shuyang Town, Nanjing County. This building is a square house, 300 years old, most of the building's descendants have moved to Taiwan.

塘深危险
请勿靠近

❶

·141·

HISTORIC HOUSES IN FUJIAN·EARTHEN BUILDING
福建经典古民居·土楼
BUILDING

109 — 174

NANJING
南靖

TIANZHONG VILLAGE SHUYANG TOWN
书洋镇田中村

❶

LONGTAN BUILDING
龙潭楼

福建经典古民居·土楼
HISTORIC HOUSES
IN FUJIAN · EARTHEN
BUILDING

109 — 174

南靖
NANJING

书洋镇大坝村
DABA VILLAGE
SHUYANG TOWN

❶
和兴楼
HEXING
BUILDING

❷
文选楼
WENXUAN
BUILDING

❸
大坝土楼
DABA'S
EARTHEN
BUILDINGS

· 143 ·

HISTORIC HOUSES IN FUJIAN · EARTHEN BUILDING
福建经典古民居·土楼

109 — 174

NANJING
南靖

DABA VILLAGE SHUYANG TOWN
书洋镇大坝村

④

QINGDE BUILDING
庆德楼

⑤

JIXING BUILDING
积兴楼

⑥

YAODONG BUILDING
耀东楼

⑦

DAOSUN BUILDING
稻孙楼

·144·

福建经典古民居·土楼
HISTORIC HOUSES
IN FUJIAN · EARTHEN
BUILDING

109 — 174

南靖
NANJING

书洋镇
SHUYANG TOWN

❶
倚峰楼
YIFENG
BUILDING

❷
朝源楼
CHAOYUAN
BUILDING

❸
圆楼
THE CIRCULAR
BUILDING

❶

❷

❸

•145•

HISTORIC HOUSES
IN FUJIAN · EARTHEN
BUILDING

福建经典古民居 · 土楼

109 — 174

南靖 NANJING

书洋镇 SHUYANG TOWN

④

三月梨花香 THE PEAR TREES IN BLOSSOM

④

·146·

福建经典古民居·土楼
HISTORIC HOUSES
IN FUJIAN·EARTHEN
BUILDING·BUILDING

109—174

南靖
NANJING

书洋镇双峰村
SHUANGFENG VILLAGE
SHUYANG TOWN

❶ ❷ ❸

灼昌楼（大寨楼）
ZHUOCHANG
BUILDINGS

·147·

HISTORIC HOUSES
IN FUJIAN · EARTHEN
BUILDING

福建经典古民居·土楼

109 — 174

南靖
NANJING

书洋镇双峰村
SHUANGFENG VILLAGE
SHUYANG TOWN

长兴楼
CHANGXING
BUILDING

❹❺

❹

❺

·148·

福建经典古民居·土楼
HISTORIC HOUSES IN FUJIAN·EARTHEN BUILDING

109 — 174
南靖
NANJING

书洋镇塔下村
TAXIA VILLAGE SHUTANG TOWN

①
塔下土楼群
TAXIA'S EARTHEN BUILDINGS

塔下土楼群（南靖）

　　位于南靖县书洋镇塔下村，最早的福兴楼建于明代崇祯四年（1631年）。后来汉人陆续建造了数座土楼，有方形、圆形、围裙形、曲尺形等等，这些土楼沿山溪呈长形摆布、千姿百态，气势恢宏。清朝末年，由于地理环境限制，塔下没有土地建造大型土楼，张姓族人便因地制宜，在沿溪两岸的空地上，又建起了一座座单院式土木、砖木结构的吊角楼，形成大楼带小楼、高低错落的奇妙景观。

①

•149•

HISTORIC HOUSES IN FUJIAN · EARTHEN BUILDING

福建经典古民居 · 土楼

109 — 174

南靖 NANJING

书洋镇塔下村 TAXIA VILLAGE SHUYANG TOWN

❶ 塔下土楼群 TAXIA'S EARTHEN BUILDINGS

Taxia's earthen buildings (Nanjing)

It is located in Taxia Village, Shuyang Town, Nanjing County. The oldest building, Fuxing Building was first built in 1631, the 4th year of Chongzhen Emperor's reign, Ming Dynasty. Later, another 42 building were built, different in shape, square, round, apron-like or trisquare. They are distributed along the river, unique in style, and structure, large in scale. At the end of Qing Dynasty, due to the geographical limit, no land could be found to build bigger building, clansmen of Zhang made full use of the open space on both sides of the river to set up many turrets. Each turret, earth-timber or brick-timber in its structure, has only one compound. A singular landscape comes into your sight: large building dotted with small building, high and low buildings interspersed.

·150·

福建经典古民居·土楼
HISTORIC HOUSES
IN FUJIAN·EARTHEN
BUILDING

109 — 174

南靖
NANJING

书洋镇塔下村
TAXIA VILLAGE
SHUYANG TOWN

❶ ❷
塔下土楼群
TAXIA'S
EARTHEN
BUILDINGS

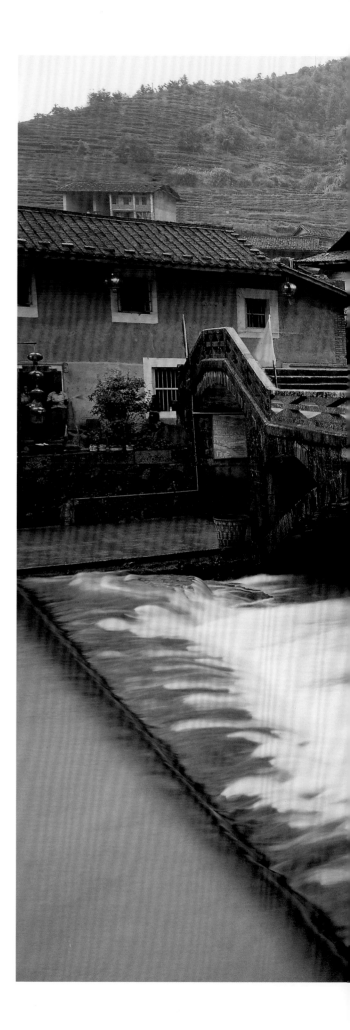

·151·

HISTORIC HOUSES
IN FUJIAN · EARTHEN
BUILDING

福建经典古民居·土楼

109 — 174

NANJING
南靖

TAXIA VILLAGE
SHUYANG TOWN
书洋镇塔下村

❸

TAXIA'S
EARTHEN
BUILDINGS
塔下土楼群

福建经典古民居·土楼
HISTORIC HOUSES
IN FUJIAN · EARTHEN
BUILDING

109 — 174

南靖
NANJING

书洋镇塔下村
TAXIA VILLAGE
SHUYANG TOWN

❶ 追继堂
ANCESTOR'S
MEMORIAL
HALL

❷ 祭祖
ANCESTOR
WORSHIP

·153·

HISTORIC HOUSES
IN FUJIAN · EARTHEN
BUILDING
福建经典古民居·土楼

109 — 174

南靖
NANJING

书洋镇塔下村
TAXIA VILLAGE
SHUYANG TOWN

❸

祭祖
ANCESTOR
WORSHIP

❸

·154·

福建经典古民居·土楼
HISTORIC HOUSES
IN FUJIAN · EARTHEN
BUILDING

109 — 174

南靖
NANJING

梅林镇长教村
CHANGJIAO VILLAGE
MEILIN TOWN

❶

怀远楼
HUAIYUAN
BUILDING

❶

怀远楼（南靖）

　　位于南靖县梅林镇长教村。建于清宣统元年（1909年），楼高四层，楼内直径33米，每层34个房间，夯筑技术炉火纯青。怀远楼天井中间的"斯是室"，既是祖堂又是私塾，正面对着大楼门，十分引人注目。

Huaiyuan Building (Nanjing)

　　Located in Changjiao Village, Meilin Town, NanJing County, this was built in 1907. Each of its four stories has 34 rooms. The interior of the building is 33 meters in diameter. The rammed-earth construction shows a high degree of professional proficiency. The room in the middle of the courtyard is both an ancestral hall and a private school. Facing the building's entrance, it attracts people's attention.

·155·

HISTORIC HOUSES IN FUJIAN·EARTHEN BUILDING
福建经典古民居·土楼

109 — 174

NANJING
南靖

CHANGJIAO VILLAGE MEILIN TOWN
梅林镇长教村

HUAIYUAN BUILDING
❷ 怀远楼

·156·

福建经典古民居·土楼
HISTORIC HOUSES
IN FUJIAN · EARTHEN
BUILDING

109 — 174

南靖
NANJING

梅林镇长教村
CHANGJIAO VILLAGE
MEILIN TOWN

❶

怀远楼
HUAIYUAN
BUILDING

·157·

HISTORIC HOUSES
IN FUJIAN · EARTHEN
BUILDING

福建经典古民居·土楼

109 — 174

南靖
NANJING

梅林镇长教村
CHANGJIAO VILLAGE
MEILIN TOWN

❷❸❹

怀远楼
HUAIYUAN
BUILDING

·158·

福建经典古民居·土楼
HISTORIC HOUSES
IN FUJIAN·EARTHEN
BUILDING

109 — 174

南靖
NANJING

梅林镇长教村
CHANGJIAO VILLAGE
MEILIN TOWN

❶

长教土楼群
CHANGJIAO'S
EARTHEN
BUILDINGS

·159·

HISTORIC HOUSES IN FUJIAN · EARTHEN BUILDING
福建经典古民居·土楼

109 — 174

南靖
NANJING

梅林镇长教村
CHANGJIAO VILLAGE MEILIN TOWN

❷❸

长教土楼群
CHANGJIAO'S EARTHEN BUILDINGS

·160·

福建经典古民居·土楼
HISTORIC HOUSES
IN FUJIAN · EARTHEN
BUILDING

109 — 174

南靖
NANJING

梅林镇璞山村
PUSHAN VILLAGE
MEILIN TOWN

❶

和贵楼
HEGUI
BUILDING

❶

和贵楼（南靖）

　　位于南靖县梅林镇璞山村。和贵楼五层，高21.5米，为已知的所有福建土楼之最。它建于沼泽地上，神奇非凡。

Hegui Building (Nanjing)

　　This is located in Pushan Village, Meilin Town, Nanjing County. At five stories and 21.5 meters high, it is the highest of all the Fujian earthen buildings. It is miraculous that it was built on swampland.

·161·

HISTORIC HOUSES IN FUJIAN · EARTHEN BUILDING

福建经典古民居 · 土楼

109 — 174

NANJING

南靖

PUSHAN VILLAGE MEILIN TOWN

梅林镇璞山村

❷

HEGUI BUILDING

和贵楼

❷

·162·

福建经典古民居·土楼
HISTORIC HOUSES
IN FUJIAN·EARTHEN
BUILDING

109—174

南靖
NANJING

梅林镇璞山村
PUSHAN VILLAGE
MEILIN TOWN

❶
和贵楼
HEGUI
BUILDING

❶

·163·

HISTORIC HOUSES
IN FUJIAN · EARTHEN
BUILDING

福建经典古民居·土楼

109 — 174

南靖
NANJING

梅林镇璞山村
PUSHAN VILLAGE
MEILIN TOWN

❷❸❹❺

和贵楼
HEGUI
BUILDING

·164·

福建经典古民居·土楼
HISTORIC HOUSES
IN FUJIAN · EARTHEN
BUILDING

109 — 174
南靖
NANJING

梅林镇璞山村
PUSHAN VILLAGE
MEILIN TOWN

❶ ❷ ❸

和贵楼
HEGUI
BUILDING

❶

❷

❸

·165·

HISTORIC HOUSES
IN FUJIAN · EARTHEN
BUILDING

福建经典古民居·土楼

109 — 174

NANJING

南靖

PUSHAN VILLAGE
MEILIN TOWN

梅林镇璞山村

❹

HEGUI
BUILDINGS

和贵楼

❹

·166·

福建经典古民居·土楼

HISTORIC HOUSES IN FUJIAN · EARTHEN BUILDING

109 — 174

南靖 NANJING

梅林镇磜头村 QITOU VILLAGE MEILIN TOWN

❶ ❷ ❸ 磜头土楼群 QITOU'S EARTHEN BUILDINGS

磜头土楼群（南靖）

　　位于南靖县梅林镇磜头村，4座圆楼3座方楼手拉手似的挽在一起，从山上往下看，犹如七星伴月，令人遐想无穷。

Qitou's Earthen Buildings (Nanjing)

　　Located in the Qitou Village,Meilin Town,Nanjing County, this building group consists of four round houses and three square houses linking hand in hand with a semicircular building.The whole group looks like seven stars in companion with the moon when looked down from the hill.

·167·

HISTORIC HOUSES
IN FUJIAN · EARTHEN
BUILDING

福建经典古民居·土楼

109 — 174

NANJING

南靖

QITOU'S VILLAGE
MEILIN TOWN

梅林镇磜头村

❹

QITOU'S
EARTHEN
BUILDINGS

磜头土楼群

·168·

福建经典古民居·土楼
HISTORIC HOUSES IN FUJIAN·EARTHEN BUILDING

109 — 174

南靖
NANJING

南坑镇新罗村
XINLUO VILLAGE NANKENG TOWN

❶

新罗土楼
XINLUO'S EARTHEN BUILDINGS

❶

·169·

HISTORIC HOUSES
IN FUJIAN · EARTHEN
BUILDING
福建经典古民居·土楼

109 — 174

南靖
NANJING

南坑镇新罗村
XINLUO VILLAGE
NANKENG TOWN

❷

半月楼
BANYUE
BUILDING

半月楼（南靖）

　　位于南靖县南坑镇新罗村，形状像一弓美丽的弯月，故称半月楼。半月楼楼前有一片平坦干净的水泥地面，前进是平房25间，后进是两层楼，一共75个房间。

Banyue Building (Nanjing)

　　It is located in Xinluo Village, Nankeng Town, Nanjing County. It looks like a beautiful bowed moon, hence comes its name. There is a piece of flat and cemented ground in front of the building, fairly clean. The front part of building is bungalow with 25 rooms, the rear has two stories with 75 rooms.

·170·

福建经典古民居·土楼
HISTORIC HOUSES
IN FUJIAN·EARTHEN
BUILDING

109 — 174

南靖
NANJING

南坑镇新罗村
XINLUO VILLAGE
NANKENG TOWN

❶
翠林楼
CUILIN
BUILDING

翠林楼（南靖）

　　位于南靖县南坑镇新罗村。建于明代嘉靖年间，楼高3层8米，楼内直径仅有9米，为目前发现的最小的土楼。

Cuilin Building (Nanjing)

Located in Xinluo Village, Nankeng Town, Nanjing County. It was built during Jiajing Emperor's reign, Ming Dynasty. This building has 3 stories, about 8 meters high, 9 meters in diameter. It is the smallest building ever discovered.

HISTORIC HOUSES
IN FUJIAN · EARTHEN
BUILDING

福建经典古民居·土楼

109 — 174

南靖
NANJING

南坑镇新罗村
XINLUO VILLAGE
NANKENG TOWN

❷❸❹❺

翠林楼
CUILIN
BUILDING

❷ ❸ ❹

❺

•172•

福建经典古民居·土楼
HISTORIC HOUSES IN FUJIAN·EARTHEN BUILDING

109 — 174

南靖
NANJING

船场镇下山村
XIASHAN VILLAGE CHUANCHANG TOWN

❶ 福兴楼
FUXING BUILDING

❷ 隆兴楼
LONGXING BUILDING

福兴楼 隆兴楼（南靖）

　　位于南靖县船场镇下山村，建于耸起的山地上，两楼隔壑相望。在高地上建土楼，较为罕见。这两座建在山上的土楼，以前都只有一条山路可以通到楼前，现在人们另外铺设了一条石阶路，从山下往上望去，它们像是旧时绿林好汉占山为王而修筑的城堡，高峻险要，易守难攻。

Fuxing Building Longxing Building (Nanjing)

　　Located in Xiashan Village, Chuanchang Town, Nanjing County, these two buildings were built on high mountain area. Separated by a ravine, they look at each other. It is rarely seen that a building is built on highland. In old days, there was only one pathway to these two buildings. nowadays, a new stone-stair road was paved. When vertical viewed, they are like bastilles set up by brigands, high and steep, easy to defend and difficult to attack.

❶

❷

•173•

HISTORIC HOUSES
IN FUJIAN · EARTHEN
BUILDING

福建经典古民居·土楼

109 — 174

NANJING

南靖

XIASHAN VILLAGE
CHUANCHANG TOWN

船场镇下山村

❸

LONGXING
BUILDING

隆兴楼

·174·

福建经典古民居·土楼
HISTORIC HOUSES IN FUJIAN·EARTHEN BUILDING

109 — 174

南靖
NANJING

船场镇下山村
XIASHAN VILLAGE
CHUANCHANG TOWN

❶❷❸
隆兴楼
LONGXING
BUILDING

华安县原属龙溪，1928年析置。为这块古老的土地，文化积淀丰厚，早在商周时期便有人类生息繁衍，仙字潭摩崖石刻是先民们劳动与创造的真实记录。

华安土楼数量不多，现存68座，主要分布在仙都镇、沙建镇、高车乡、高安镇等，其中仙都镇大地村的二宜楼为最杰出的代表，是最早列入全国重点文物保护单位的土楼。华安土楼与永定、南靖土楼最大的不同，在于它多为单元式，以单个开间或多开间为一个独立单元，每个单元各自有单独的出入口、小天井和独用的楼梯，具有较强的私密性。华安土楼形式的演变也为反映出闽南人在维系家族纽带的同时，更加注重居住空间的私密性、独立性与舒适性。华安土楼的另一个重要特色是大多有碑刻纪年。在华安沙建镇的上坪村，现存六幢明清时代建造的土楼均有准确的建造纪年。齐云楼，明万历十八年（1590年）；昇平楼，清康熙二十二年（1683年）；日新楼，明万历三十一年（1603年）；月升楼，清康熙二十二年（1683年）；文洋楼，清乾隆五十年（1785年）；凌云楼，清同治四年（1865年）。

同为漳州市管辖的平和县、漳浦县、诏安县和云霄县，也有数量不等的土楼，多为客家人所建，主要也是单元式，其中漳浦县的一德楼，为方形土楼，碑刻记载建于明嘉靖三十七年（1558年）。又如锦江楼，这座三环式土楼第一环平房，第二环两层，第三环三层，从外到内一环比一环高，和永定、南靖土楼截然相反，远远看去，整座楼就像金字塔一样，表现出一种不同凡响的气势。平和土楼，著名的有绳武楼、丰作厥宁楼等。绳武楼的独特价值和无尽魅力在于装饰的精美绝伦，屋瓦上、门窗上、墙壁上，到处是泥塑、石雕、木雕和壁画，仅仅木雕就有600多处。既有人物花草、文字对联，又有飞禽走兽和各种物品，诗画结合，动静相宜，竟无一处雷同，被专家称为一木雕博物馆。

福建土楼申报世界文化遗产时，平和的绳武楼、漳浦的锦江楼未能一同列入，不免让人遗憾。

闽南的永春、安溪、同安等地也有一些土楼，它们和华安土楼较为接近，显示了土楼在传播中的变异。

FUJIAN'S EARTHEN BUILDINGS

HUA'AN AND OTHER PLACES

Hua'an county wasn't established until 1928, but culture flourished here as early as the Shang and Zhou dynasties. The ancient rock carving in Xianzitan attests to the human work and creativity that were long ago present here.Hua'an doesn't have many earthen buildings; there are only 68 extant, with most located in Xiandu town, Shajian town, Gaoche village, and Gao'an town. Of these, the Eryi building in Dadi village, Xiandu town, is the best example; it was the first earthen building to be accorded state protection as a cultural relic. The greatest difference between Hua'an's earthen buildings and those in Yongding and Nanjing is that Hua'an's are mostly single units of one room or several rooms. Each unit has its own entrance, small courtyard, and separate staircase; thus, each one is relatively private. Although Hua'an county is made up of southern Fujian people, records show that many of the clans came from Hakka regions. The different style of the earthen buildings here shows that, although the southern Fujian people placed the major emphasis on clan ties, they also placed more value than the Hakka did on the privacy, independence, and comfort associated with their housing. Another important characteristic of the Hua'an earthen buildings is that most have annals engraved on steles. In Shangping village, Shajian town, six extant Ming and Qing dynasty earthen buildings have such steles: Qiyun Building (1590); Shengping Building (1601), Rixin Building (1603); Yuesheng Building (1683); Wenyang Building (1785); and Lingyun Building (1865).

Pinghe, Zhangpu, Zhao'an, and Yunxiao counties also have earthen buildings, most built by the Hakka. They are also mostly single-unit buildings, among them the square Yide building in Zhangpu county, constructed—according to its stele—in 1558. The first ring of the three-ring Jinjiang building is a one-story house, the second ring is two stories, and the third is three stories. Thus, each of the rings is successively higher, completely opposite from the earthen buildings in Yongding and Nanjing. Looked at from a distance, the Jinjiang building is unusually impressive. In Pinghe county, the most famous earthen buildings are the Shengwu and the Juening. Shengwu's unique value and unparalleled charm lie in its exquisite interior decoration. Clay sculptures, wood carvings, and murals are everywhere—on the roofs, doors, windows, and walls. Wooden carvings decorate more than 600 places in this building. These include images of people and plants, literary couplets, birds and beasts, and other decorative objects, none duplicating any of the others. Experts call it "a museum of wooden carvings".

Unfortunately, when earthen buildings from Yongding, Nanjing, and Hua'an were nominated for World Cultural Heritage status, Pinghe's Shengwu building and Zhangpu's Jinjiang building couldn't yet be included. This was disappointing. They could be included in a future nomination, however.

In recent years, earthen buildings have also been discovered in Yongchun, Anxi, Tong'an, and other places. They are rather close in style to Hua'an's earthen buildings, thus showing the variations through diffusion of the earthen buildings.

·177·

HISTORIC HOUSES IN FUJIAN · EARTHEN BUILDING

福建经典古民居 · 土楼

175 — 193

HUA'AN

华安

DADI VILLAGE XIANDU TOWN

仙都镇大地村

❶ ❷

ERYI BUILDING

二宜楼

二宜楼（华安）

　　位于华安县仙都镇大地村。依山傍水，占地6666平方米，外环楼四层，内环楼单层，分成12单元。土楼的内部装饰一般比较简朴，但二宜楼是个例外，不但雕梁画栋，更有诗书题壁，人物花鸟彩绘，特别奢华，犹如一座精美的艺术殿堂。

Eryi Building (Hua'an)

　　This is located in Dadi Village, Xiandu Town, Hua'an County. It occupies nearly 6666 square meters of land. Mountains stand behind it and a river runs alongside it. It comprises a four-story outer ring and a single-story inner ring, and is divided into twelve units. The interior decorations in most earthen buildings are relatively simple, but Eryi Building is an exception. Not only are there carved girders and painted ridgepoles, but walls are inscribed with poetry and calligraphy. The colorful drawings of people, flowers, and birds are extravagantlike a museum of exquisite craftsmanship.

•178•

福建经典古民居·土楼
HISTORIC HOUSES
IN FUJIAN · EARTHEN
BUILDING

175 — 193

华安
HUA'AN

仙都镇大地村
DADI VILLAGE
XIANDU TOWN

❶❷

二宜楼
ERYI
BUILDING

❶

❷

③

④

·179·

HISTORIC HOUSE
IN FUJIAN · EARTHEN
BUILDING

福建经典古民居 · 土楼

175 — 193

HUA AN

华安

DADI VILLAGE
XIANDU TOWN

仙都镇大地村

③④⑤

KUIJU
BUILDING

二宜楼

⑤

·180·

福建经典古民居·土楼
HISTORIC HOUSES IN FUJIAN · EARTHEN BUILDING

175 — 193

华安
HUA AN

仙都镇大地村
DADI VILLAGE XIANDU TOWN

二宜楼
ERYI BUILDING

❶

❷

❶❷❸

❸

·181·

HISTORIC HOUSES IN FUJIAN · EARTHEN BUILDING

福建经典古民居·土楼

175 — 193

HUA AN

华安

DADI VILLAGE XIANDU TOWN

仙都镇大地村

❹❺❻

ERYI BUILDING

二宜楼

·182·

福建经典古民居 · 土楼
HISTORIC HOUSES
IN FUJIAN · EARTHEN
BUILDING

175 — 193

华安
HUA'AN

仙都镇大地村
DADI VILLAGE
XIANDU TOWN

①②③④

二宜楼
ERYI
BUILDING

①

②

③

④

·183·

HISTORIC HOUSES
IN FUJIAN · EARTHEN
BUILDING

福建经典古民居·土楼

175 — 193

HUA AN
华安

DADI VILLAGE
XIANDU TOWN
仙都镇大地村

⑤⑥

ERYI
BUILDING
二宜楼

⑤

⑥

福建经典古民居·土楼
HISTORIC HOUSES
IN FUJIAN·EARTHEN
BUILDING

175 — 193

华安
HUA AN

仙都镇大地村
DADI VILLAGE
XIANDU TOWN

❶❷❸

二宜楼
ERYI
BUILDING

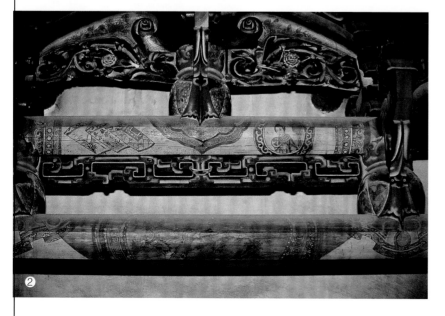

④

⑦

⑤

⑥

⑧

·185·

HISTORIC HOUSES
IN FUJIAN · EARTHEN
BUILDING
福建经典古民居·土楼

175—193

HUA AN
华安

DADI VILLAGE
XIANDU TOWN
仙都镇大地村

④⑤
⑥⑦⑧

ERYI
BUILDING
二宜楼

·186·

福建经典古民居·土楼
HISTORIC HOUSES
IN FUJIAN·EARTHEN
BUILDING

175 — 193

华安
HUA AN

仙都镇大地村
DADI VILLAGE
XIANDU TOWN

❶ ❷
❸ ❹ ❺

二宜楼
ERYI
BUILDING

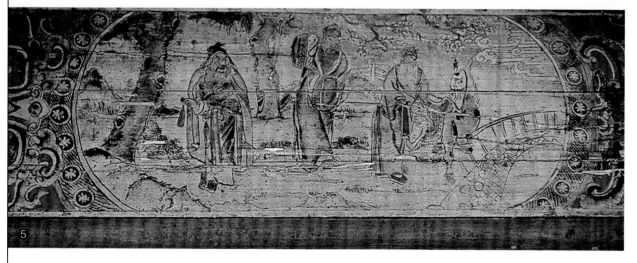

•187•

HISTORIC HOUSES
IN FUJIAN · EARTHEN
BUILDING

福建经典古民居·土楼

175 — 193

华安

HUA'AN

仙都镇大地村

DADI VILLAGE
XIANDU TOWN

6 7 8

ERYI
BUILDING

二宜楼

•188•

福建经典古民居·土楼
HISTORIC HOUSES
IN FUJIAN
BUILDING·EARTHEN

175 — 193

华安
HUA AN

仙都镇大地村
DADI VILLAGE
XIANDU TOWN

❶

南阳楼
NANYANG
BUILDING

❶

·189·

HISTORIC HOUSES IN FUJIAN · EARTHEN BUILDING
福建经典古民居·土楼

175 — 193

华安 HUA'AN

DADI VILLAGE XIANDU TOWN 仙都镇大地村

❷❸ 东阳楼 DONGYANG BUILDING

❷ ──────────── ❸

南阳楼 东阳楼（华安）

　　位于华安县仙都镇大地村，虽无二宜楼的名气，却和它一起组成壮丽的大地土楼群。

Nanyang Building Dongyang Building (Hua'an)

　　Located in Dadi Village, Xiandu Town, Hua'an County, these two buildings are not so famous as the Eryi Building, yet with the Eryi Building, they make up a grand building group.

·190·

福建经典古民居·土楼
HISTORIC HOUSES
IN FUJIAN · EARTHEN
BUILDING

175 — 193

华安
HUA AN

沙建镇岱山村
DAISHAN VILLAGE
SHAJIAN TOWN

❶❷
齐云楼
QIYUN
BUILDING

❶

❷

齐云楼（华安）

　　位于华安县沙建镇岱山村。建于明朝万历十八年（1590年），为双环式椭圆楼，共有26个单元。除了大门以外，还在天井两端呈尖棱的位置，向北开一小门，称"死门"，向南又开一门，叫"生门"，极为少见。

Qinyun Building (Hua'an)

　　Located in Daishan Village, Shajian Town, Hua'an County, this building was built in the 18th year of Wanli Emperor's reign, Ming Dynasty. It is an ellipse building with two circles, 26 units. Besides the entrance door, a small door called "death door" was opened in the north at the two ends of the patio, in the south, a door called "living door".

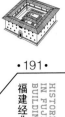

·191·

HISTORIC HOUSES
IN FUJIAN · EARTHEN
BUILDING

福建经典古民居·土楼

175— 193

HUA'AN

华安

DAISHAN VILLAGE
SHAJIAN TOWN

沙建镇岱山村

❸❹

QIYUN
BUILDING

齐云楼

·192·

福建经典古民居·土楼

HISTORIC HOUSES IN FUJIAN · EARTHEN BUILDING

175 — 193

华安

HUA'AN

高车乡洋竹径村

YANGZHUJING VILLAGE GAOCHE TOWN

❶ 雨伞楼

YUSAN BUILDINGS

雨伞楼（华安）

　　位于华安县高车乡洋竹径村，为当地蔡氏所建。通常的圆土楼，如建有内外两环，一般是外高内低，呈碗状，而雨伞楼内环比外环高一层，犹如雨伞，因此得名。

Yusan Building (Hua'an)

　　It is located in Yangzhujing Village, Gaoche Town, Hua'an County. This building was built by the Cai family. For round buildings, if it has two circles, the outer circle is usually higher than the inner circle, but in Yusan Building, inner circle like an umbrella. Hence comes the name of this building.

❶

•193•

HISTORIC HOUSES
IN FUJIAN · EARTHEN
BUILDING

福建经典古民居 · 土楼

175 — 193

HUA' AN

华安

YANGZHUJING VILLAGE
GAOCHE TOWN

高车乡洋竹径村

❶

YUSAN
BUILDING

雨伞楼

•194•

福建经典古民居·土楼
HISTORIC HOUSES IN FUJIAN·EARTHEN BUILDING

194 — 205

新罗
XINLUO

适中镇中心村
ZHONGXIN VILLAGE SHIZHONG TOWN

❶❷

典常楼
DIANCHANG BUILDING

❶

典常楼（新罗）

　　谢氏民居，又名瑞云楼，位于龙岩市新罗区适中镇中心村。它建于清乾隆四十九年（1784年），占地面积2800多平方米，其中建筑面积2526.71平方米。其结构精巧、错落有致，院中有楼、楼中有院。

Dianchang Building (Xinluo)

　　XieShi Residential House, also known as Ruiyun House, is located in Zhongxin Village, Shizhong Town, Xinluo District, Longyan City. It was built in the forty-ninth year of Qianlong Period of Qing Dynasty(1784). It occupies an area of more than 2.8 thousand square meters, including construction area of 2526.71 square meters. Compact structure, picturesque disorder, buildings in the yards, and yards in the buildings.

❷

·195·

HISTORIC HOUSES
IN FUJIAN · EARTHEN
BUILDING
福建经典古民居·土楼

194—205

新罗
XINLUO

适中镇中心村
ZHONGXIN VILLAGE
SHIZHONG TOWN

③④⑤

典常楼
DIANCHANG
BUILDING

③

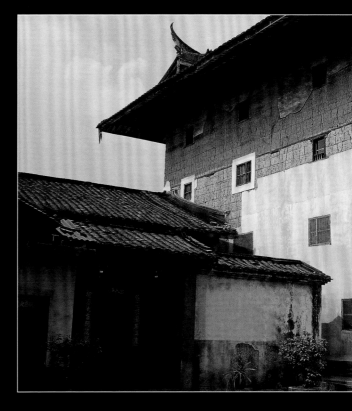

④

⑤

•196•

福建经典古民居·土楼
HISTORIC HOUSES IN FUJIAN·EARTHEN BUILDING

194—205

新罗
XINLUO

适中镇中心村
ZHONGXIN VILLAGE SHIZHONG TOWN

❶

典常楼
DIANCHANG BUILDING

❶

·197·

HISTORIC HOUSES
IN FUJIAN · EARTHEN
BUILDING
福建经典古民居·土楼

194 — 205

XINLUO
新罗

ZHONGXIN VILLAGE
SHIZHONG TOWN
适中镇中心村

❷❸❹❺

DIANCHANG
BUILDING
典常楼

·198·

福建经典古民居·土楼
HISTORIC HOUSES IN FUJIAN · EARTHEN BUILDING

194 — 205

新罗
XINLUO

适中镇中心村
ZHONGXIN VILLAGE SHIZHONG TOWN

❶

善成楼
SHANCHENG BUILDING

❶

善成楼（新罗）

　　位于龙岩市新罗区适中镇中心村，清朝嘉庆八年（1803年）建成，占地12400平方米，耗银13万。

Shancheng Building (Xinluo)

　　Located in Zhongxin Village, Shizhong Town, Xinluo Distriet, Longyan City, it was built in 1804. It occupies 12400 square meters of land, and cost 130000 silver dollars.

•199•

HISTORIC HOUSES
IN FUJIAN · EARTHEN
BUILDING

福建经典古民居·土楼

194 — 205

XINLUO
新罗

ZHONGXIN VILLAGE
SHIZHONG TOWN
适中镇中心村

❷

SHANCHENG
BUILDING
善成楼

❷

·200·

福建经典古民居·土楼
HISTORIC HOUSES
IN FUJIAN·EARTHEN
BUILDING

194 — 205

新罗
XINLUO

适中镇中心村
ZHONGXIN VILLAGE
SHIZHONG TOWN

❶

善成楼
SHANCHENG
BUILDING

·201·

HISTORIC HOUSES IN FUJIAN · EARTHEN BUILDING

福建经典古民居·土楼

194—205

新罗 XINLUO

适中镇中心村 ZHONGXIN VILLAGE SHIZHONG TOWN

❷❸ 善成楼 SHANCHENG BUILDING

❷

❸

•202•

福建经典古民居·土楼
HISTORIC HOUSES
IN FUJIAN · EARTHEN
BUILDING

194 — 205

新罗
XINLUO

适中镇中心村
ZHONGXIN VILLAGE
SHIZHONG TOWN

❶

和致楼
HEZHI
BUILDING

❶

·203·

HISTORIC HOUSES
IN FUJIAN · EARTHEN
BUILDING

福建经典古民居·土楼

194 — 205

XINLUO
新罗

ZHONGXIN VILLAGE
SHIZHONG TOWN
适中镇中心村

❷❸

QINGYUN
BUILDING
庆云楼

•204•

福建经典古民居·土楼
HISTORIC HOUSES
IN FUJIAN·EARTHEN
BUILDING

194 — 205

新罗
XINLUO

适中镇中心村
ZHONGXIN VILLAGE
SHIZHONG TOWN

❶❷

古风楼
GUFENG
BUILDING

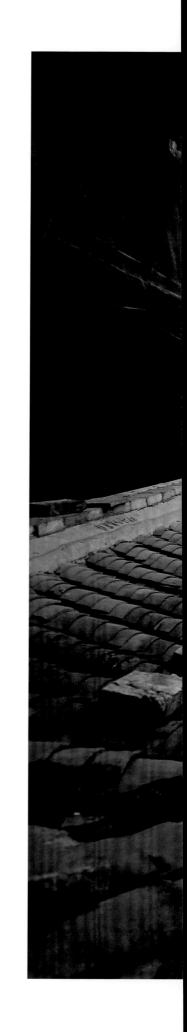

古风楼（新罗）

　　陈氏民居，位于龙岩市新罗区适中镇中心村。建于南宋建炎二年（1128年）。坐东朝西，墙高13.80米，占地面积941.69平方米，黏土夯筑。

Gufeng Building (Xinluo)

　　Chen Residential House, located in Zhongxin Village, Shizhong Town, Xinluo District, Longyan City, was built in the 2nd year of Jianyan Period in Southern Song Dynasty (1128). Taking East headed west, with walls in height of 13.80 meters, covers an area of 941.69 square meters. The buildings are made of clay–

•205•

HISTORIC HOUSES IN FUJIAN · EARTHEN BUILDING

福建经典古民居·土楼

194 — 205

XINLUO

新罗

ZHONGXIN VILLAGE SHIZHONG TOWN

适中镇中心村

❸

GUFENG BUILDING

古风楼

❸

·206·

福建经典古民居·土楼
HISTORIC HOUSES IN FUJIAN · EARTHEN BUILDING

206—225

平和
PINGHE

芦溪镇蕉路村
JIAOLU VILLAGE LUXI TOWN

❶❷❸
绳武楼
SHENGWU BUILDING

❶

❷

绳武楼（平和）

　　位于平和县芦溪镇蕉路村，由清朝太学士叶处侯在嘉庆年间投资兴建，其独特价值和无尽魅力在于内部装饰的精美绝伦，屋瓦上、门窗上、墙壁上，到处是泥塑、石雕、木雕和壁画，仅仅木雕就有600多处，既有人物花草、文字对联，又有飞禽走兽、装饰物品，诗画结合，动静相宜，竟无一处雷同，被专家称为"木雕博物馆"。

Shengwu Building (Pinghe) ———

　　Located in Jiaolu Village, Luxi Town, Pinghe County, this building was financed and built by Ye Chuhou, a scholar during the Jiaqing Emperor's reign, Qing Dynasty. Its immeasurable value and enchantment lies in its inner decoration, there are clay sculpture, stone carving, woodcarving and fresco on roof tile, windows and walls. There are over 600 woodcarvings, including human portraits, flower, couplet, birds, beasts, and ornaments. No carving was duplicated. The building is regarded as "woodcarving museum" by experts.

❸

•207•

HISTORIC HOUSES
IN FUJIAN · EARTHEN
BUILDING

福建经典古民居·土楼

206 — 225

PINGHE

平和

JIAOLU VILLAGE
LUXI TOWN

芦溪镇蕉路村

❹❺

SHENGWU
BUILDING

绳武楼

·208·

福建经典古民居·土楼
HISTORIC HOUSES
IN FUJIAN · EARTHEN
BUILDING

206 — 225

平和
PINGHE

芦溪镇蕉路村
JIAOLU VILLAGE
LUXI TOWN

❶
绳武楼
SHENGWU
BUILDING

·209·

HISTORIC HOUSES
IN FUJIAN · EARTHEN
BUILDING
福建经典古民居·土楼

206 — 225

PINGHE
平和

JIAOLU VILLAGE
LUXI TOWN
芦溪镇蕉路村

❶

SHENGWU
BUILDING
绳武楼

·210·

福建经典古民居·土楼
HISTORIC HOUSES
IN FUJIAN · EARTHEN
BUILDING

206 — 225

平和
PINGHE

芦溪镇蕉路村
JIAOLU VILLAGE
LUXI TOWN

❶❷❸
❹❺❻

绳武楼
SHENGWU
BUILDING

❶

❷

❸

❹

❺

❻

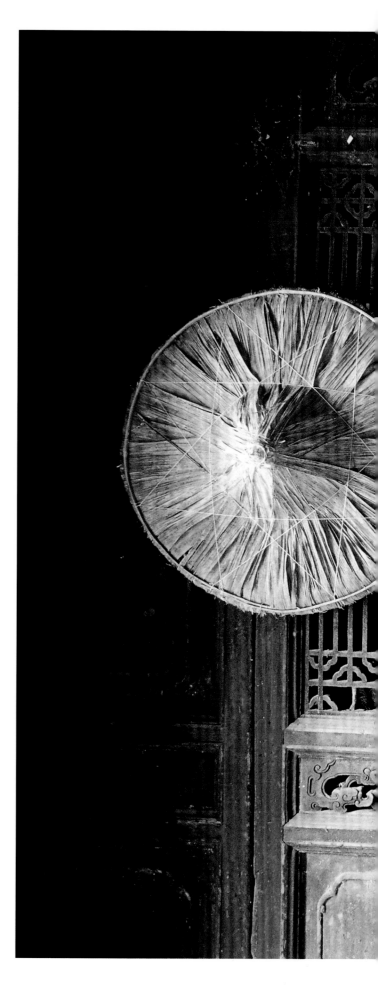

·211·

HISTORIC HOUSES
IN FUJIAN · EARTHEN
BUILDING

福建经典古民居·土楼

206 — 225

PINGHE

平和

JIAOLU VILLAGE
LUXI TOWN

芦溪镇蕉路村

❼

SHENGWU
BUILDING

绳武楼

·212·

福建经典古民居·土楼
HISTORIC HOUSES
IN FUJIAN·EARTHEN
BUILDING

206 — 225

平和
PINGHE

芦溪镇蕉路村
JIAOLU VILLAGE
LUXI TOWN

①②③

绳武楼
SHENGWU
BUILDING

•213•

HISTORIC HOUSES
IN FUJIAN · EARTHEN
BUILDING

福建经典古民居 · 土楼

206 — 225

PINGHE

平和

JIAOLU VILLAGE
LUXI TOWN

芦溪镇蕉路村

❹❺❻

SHENGWU
BUILDING

绳武楼

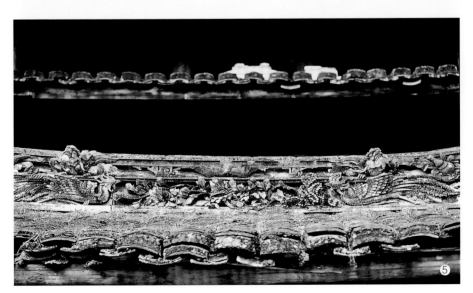

福建经典古民居·土楼
HISTORIC HOUSES
IN FUJIAN·EARTHEN
BUILDING

206 — 225

平和
PINGHE

芦溪镇蕉路村
JIAOLU VILLAGE
LUXI TOWN

① ② ③
④ ⑤ ⑥

绳武楼（上图）
SHENGWU
BUILDING

②

③

①

⑦

⑧

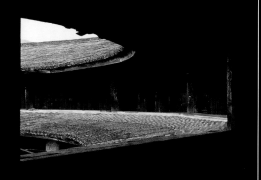

·215·

HISTORIC HOUSES
IN FUJIAN · EARTHEN
BUILDING

福建经典古民居·土楼

206 — 225

PINGHE

平和

JIAOLU VILLAGE
LUXI TOWN

芦溪镇蕉路村

❼ ❽
❾ ❿ ⓫

SHENGWU
BUILDING

绳武楼（下图）

·216·

福建经典古民居·土楼
HISTORIC HOUSES
IN FUJIAN·EARTHEN
BUILDING

206 — 225

平和
PINGHE

芦溪镇蕉路村
JIAOLU VILLAGE
LUXI TOWN

❶❷❸

丰作厥宁楼
FENZUOJUENING
BUILDING

丰作厥宁楼（平和）

　　位于平和县芦溪镇蕉路村。这是闽西南土楼直径最大的圆楼，直径达77米。楼高四层，每层72间，一共288个房间。站在宽敞的天井，环顾四周，可以感受到什么叫气势。楼内每家每户都有一座门楼，一个小天井以及自家的楼梯，相对而言更加独立和私密。

Fengzuojuening Building (Pinghe)

　　This is located in Jiaolu Village, Luxi Town, Pinghe County. This is the largest circular earthen building in diameter. Standing in the spacious patio and looking around, you may understand the real meaning of grandeur.

•217•

HISTORIC HOUSES IN FUJIAN·EARTHEN BUILDING

福建经典古民居·土楼

206 — 225

PINGHE 平和

JIAOLU VILLAGE LUXI TOWN 芦溪镇蕉路村

❹❺
❻❼

FENZUOJUENING BUILDING 丰作厥宁楼

·218·

福建经典古民居·土楼
HISTORIC HOUSES
IN FUJIAN·EARTHEN
BUILDING · BUILDING

206 — 225

平和
PINGHE

芦溪镇蕉路村
JIAOLU VILLAGE
LUXI TOWN

❶

丰作厥宁楼
FENGZUOQUENING
BUILDING

·219·

HISTORIC HOUSES IN FUJIAN · EARTHEN BUILDING
福建经典古民居·土楼

206 — 225

平和
PINGHE

芦溪镇蕉路村
JIAOLU VILLAGE LUXI TOWN

❶

丰作厥宁楼
FENGZUOJUENING BUILDINGS

1

·220·

福建经典古民居·土楼
HISTORIC HOUSES IN FUJIAN·EARTHEN BUILDING

206 — 225

平和
PINGHE

霞寨镇西安村
XI'AN VILLAGE XIAZHAI TOWN

①②

西爽楼
XISHUANG BUILDING

西爽楼（平和）

　　位于平和县霞寨镇西安村，大型方楼，已有400年历史，楼内天井房屋层叠，错综复杂，犹如庞大村落。

Xishuang Building (Pinghe)

　　It is located in Xi'an Village, Xiazhai Town, Pinghe County. This square house has a history of 400 years. The patios and rooms inside the building were built row by row to have formed a massive village.

•221•

HISTORIC HOUSES
IN FUJIAN · EARTHEN
BUILDING
福建经典古民居·土楼

206 — 225

PINGHE
平和

XIAN VILLAGE
XIAZHAI TOWN
霞寨镇西安村

❸ ❹ ❺

XISHUANG
BUILDING
西爽楼

·222·

福建经典古民居·土楼
HISTORIC HOUSES IN FUJIAN · EARTHEN BUILDING

206 — 225

平和
PINGHE

大溪镇庄上村
ZHUANGSHANG VILLAGE DAXI TOWN

❶❷❸❹

庄上楼
ZHUANGSHANG BUILDING

庄上土楼（平和）

　　位于平和县大溪镇庄上村。中国最大方型土楼——庄上土楼，建于清代顺治至康熙年间，南北相距220米，周长700多米，楼高9米，占地34650平方米；环山而建，楼中有山，是其最大特色。

Zhuangshang Building (Pinghe)

　　It is located in Zhuangshang Village, Daxi Town, Pinghe County.　China's largest square Tulou—Zhuangshang Building, was built during the period of Shunzhi and Kangxi in Qing dynasty, 220 meters between the North and the South, more than 700 meters in circumference, 9 meters in height, it occupies an area of 34,650 square meters.　However, being built at the foot of mountains and also some mountains hidden among the houses, is its most significant feature.

•223•

HISTORIC HOUSES IN FUJIAN · EARTHEN BUILDING
福建经典古民居 · 土楼

206—225

PINGHE
平和

ZHUANGSHANG VILLAGE DAXI TOWN
大溪镇庄上村

⑤⑥
⑦⑧⑨

ZHUANGSHANG BUILDING
庄上土楼

福建经典古民居·土楼
HISTORIC HOUSES
IN FUJIAN·EARTHEN
BUILDING

206 — 225

平和
PINGHE

大溪镇庄上村
ZHUANGSHANG VILLAGE
DAXI TOWN

❶
❷❸❹

庄上土楼
ZHUANGSHANG
BUILDING

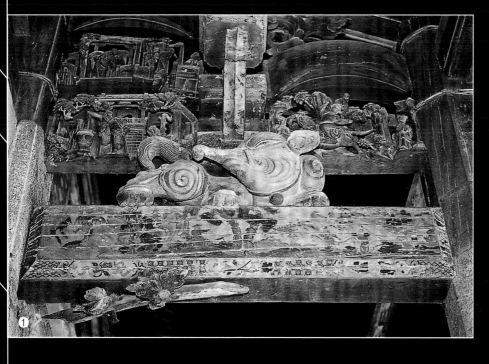

·225·

HISTORIC HOUSES
IN FUJIAN · EARTHEN
BUILDING

福建经典古民居·土楼

206—225

平和
PINGHE

坂仔镇东风村
DONGFENG VILLAGE
BANZI TOWN

⑤⑥⑦⑧

薰南楼
XUNNAN
BUILDING

⑤

⑥

⑦

⑧

·226·

HISTORIC HOUSES
IN FUJIAN · EARTHEN
BUILDING

福建经典古民居 · 土楼

226 — 226

诏安
ZHAO'AN

官陂镇大边村
DABIAN VILLAGE
GUANPI TOWN

❶

在田楼
ZAITIAN
BUILDING

❶

在田楼（诏安）

　　位于诏安县官陂镇大边村。建于清乾隆年间，是现存最大的八卦楼，直径94.5米，楼高三层12米。主楼分为八卦，即八大单元。每卦8个开间，全楼八卦64个开间，与八卦推演完全一致。与主楼相连的内环平房也分为八卦，每卦5开间。

Zaitian Building (Zhao'an)

　　Located in Dabian Village, Guanpi Town, Zhao'an County, and built during the Qianlong Emperor's reign, Qing Dynasty, this building is the largest Eight Diagram building ever known. It has three stories, about 12 meters high, 94.5 meters in diameter. The main tower is divided into eight diagrams, i.e 8 units. Each diagram is subdivided into yet another eight diagrams with 8 rooms each. So, the whole building has 64 diagrams and 64 rooms. The building is divided exactly according to the Eight Diagrams. The bungalow connected with the main tower is also divided into eight diagrams, with 5 rooms for each diagram.

·227·

HISTORIC HOUSES IN FUJIAN · EARTHEN BUILDING

福建经典古民居·土楼

227—229

漳浦 ZHANGPU

深土镇东平村 DONGPING VILLAGE SHENTU TOWN

❷

八卦堡 BAGUA BUILDING

❷

八卦堡（漳浦）

　　位于漳浦县深土镇东平村，建造时间是清代中期，至今约300年，跟一般土楼相比，它没有封闭，而完全是敞开的。从高处往下看，八卦堡围绕同一圆心，环环相套共有五环平房。中间是一座完整的圆楼，只有14间大小均匀的房间。

Bagua Building (Zhangpu)

　　It is located in Dongping Village, Shentu Town, Zhangpu County. This building was built in the middle of Qing Dynasty, about three hundred years ago. Compared with the other buildings, this building is totally open. Looked down, this eight diagrams fortress is surrounded with the center of the same circle, one circle is connected with another one, and the whole fortress has five circles. In the center, there is a round building with 14 rooms of the same size.

·228·

福建经典古民居·土楼
HISTORIC HOUSES
IN FUJIAN · EARTHEN
BUILDING

227 — 229

漳浦
ZHANGPU

深土镇锦东村
JINDONG VILLAGE
SHENTU TOWN

❶

锦江楼
JINJIANG
BUILDING

❶

锦江楼（漳浦）

　　位于漳浦县深土镇锦东村。为三环式圆楼，内环比外环高，类似金字塔，造型独特。

Jinjiang Building (Zhangpu)

　　Located in Jingdong Village, Shentu Town, Zhangpu County, this is a three-circle round building. Its outer circle is higher than inner circle, so the building looks a pyramid with its peculiar structure.

·229·

HISTORIC HOUSES
IN FUJIAN · EARTHEN
BUILDING

福建经典古民居·土楼

227 — 229

漳浦

ZHANGPU

深土镇锦东村

JINDONG VILLAGE
SHENTU TOWN

②③

锦江楼

JINJIANG
BUILDING

·230·

福建经典古民居·土楼
HISTORIC HOUSES IN FUJIAN · EARTHEN BUILDING

230 — 231

云霄
YUNXIAO

火田镇菜埔村
CAIPU VILLAGE HUOTIAN TOWN

❶❷❸

菜埔堡
CAIPU BUILDING

菜埔堡（云霄）

　　位于云霄县火田镇菜埔村。已建400余年，当地人俗称"城内"。椭圆形，四周原有护城河环绕，辟有东西南北四门。现在城里尚有年代久远的广场、府第以及杂乱的新建筑。

Caipu Building (Yunxiao)

　　Located in Caipu Village, Huotian Town, Yunxiao County, this building was built four hundred years ago and called "inner town" by the locals. This castle is oval, and there is a river guarding the house. It has four gates for east, west, south and north side. There were old plaza, mansion and new buildings in the building.

•231•

HISTORIC HOUSES IN FUJIAN · EARTHEN BUILDING
福建经典古民居 · 土楼

230 — 231

YUNXIAO
云霄

CAIPU VILLAGE HUOTIAN TOWN
火田镇菜埔村

❹❺
❻❼❽

CAIPU BUILDING
菜埔堡

·232·

福建经典古民居·土楼
HISTORIC HOUSES
IN FUJIAN · EARTHEN
BUILDING

232 — 233

三明
SANMING

❶

三明土楼群
SANMING'S
EARTHEN
BUILDINGS

❶

·233·

HISTORIC HOUSES IN FUJIAN · EARTHEN BUILDING

福建经典古民居·土楼

232 — 233

三明 SANMING

❷ ❸

三明土楼群 SANMING'S EARTHEN BUILDINGS

·234·

福建经典古民居·土楼

HISTORIC HOUSES
IN FUJIAN·EARTHEN
BUILDING

234 — 238

❶ ❷ ❸

民俗

FOLK·CUSTOM

·235·

HISTORIC HOUSES
IN FUJIAN · EARTHEN
BUILDING

福建经典古民居·土楼

234 — 238

❹

FOLK-CUSTOM

民俗

❹

·236·

福建经典古民居·土楼
HISTORIC HOUSES
IN FUJIAN · EARTHEN
BUILDING

234 — 238

❶

民俗
FOLK-CUSTOM

①

·237·

HISTORIC HOUSES
IN FUJIAN · EARTHEN
BUILDING

福建经典古民居 · 土楼

234 — 238

②

民俗

FOLK-CUSTOM

·238·

福建经典古民居·土楼

HISTORIC HOUSES
IN FUJIAN · EARTHEN
BUILDING

234 — 238

❶

民俗

FOLK-CUSTOM

❶